HAIL TO THE CHIEF!

10

QUESTIONS
to ask every
OVAL OFFICE
CANDIDATE

HAIL TO THE CHIEF!

10

QUESTIONS

to ask every

OVAL OFFICE

CANDIDATE

DONNA CAROL VOSS

V

VANTAGES
BOOKS

V
VANTAGES
BOOKS

VANTAGES BOOKS, LLC
Kaysville, UT 84037
www.vantagesbooks.com

Design by GKS Creative, Nashville

FIRST EDITION

ISBN 978-0-9906226-3-5

"Read widely and think for yourself."

—Camille Paglia

CONTENTS

INTRODUCTION

SEVERAL YEARS AGO, I HAD A CONVERSATION with a family friend from Denmark. We were talking about our respective countries when I said, "I'm proud to be an American." I'll never forget his response. He looked at me with all seriousness and said, "You should re-think that."

Clearly, he didn't know America the way I know America.

I have no illusions about our faults, our shortcomings, our mistakes, or our sins, if you will. America is the worst country there is—except for all the others. We in this country hit the best nation jackpot, and I give thanks every day that I am lucky enough to live here.

Not only am I lucky to be an American, I am shooting stars lucky to be a 21st Century Woman in America. I have more freedom, more opportunity, and more power here than I would anywhere else on the planet. Together, my sister 21st Century Women and I have enormous power to affect our world. We are the majority of citizens and the majority of voters; we can absolutely rock the 2016 presidential election.

Not only am I lucky to be an American, I am shooting stars lucky to be a 21st Century Woman in America.

As we approach the election, it is our privilege and responsibility to evaluate the candidates effectively. To do so, we have to be clear about our own personal values and how they shape our vision for the country; accordingly we are then able to evaluate the candidates' vision for the country.

It's time to pick sides. There's no middle ground left, and the waters are rising. If you've hesitated to move definitively left or definitively right, know that your cozy cocoon of moderate is virtually extinct. Today there are two ships and no communication between them. It's an all or nothing ride. If you support, let's say, Black Lives Matter[1], your political positions automatically converge on the "intersectional" axis, i.e., you can't talk about racism apart from sexism, apart from homophobia, apart from … you get my drift. Likewise if you find yourself agreeing with The Federalist[2], you are automatically presumed racist, homophobic, sexist, Islamophobic, and a product of white privilege.

It is our privilege and responsibility to evaluate the candidates effectively. To do so, we have to be clear about our own personal values and how they shape our vision for the country; accordingly we are then able to evaluate the candidates' vision for the country.

The short-term requirement is to pick a side. The long term requirement is to recognize how such polemical views polarize our society and gridlock

---

1 The website for Black Lives Matter; BlackLivesMatter.com

2 The website for the Federalist; TheFederalist.com

our government. We're so angry at each other that we too often vote from emotion rather than intellect, which knee-jerk reactions have brought us to the mess we're in now.

The long term requirement is to recognize how such polemical views polarize our society and gridlock our government. We're so angry at each other that we too often vote from emotion rather than intellect.

We're going to elect a new president this year and every four years thereafter. It is cool, rational thought that allows us to discern which candidates are divisive and which are unifying; which will uphold the Constitution and which will use power as the means to an end; which will spend our treasure wisely and which will buy votes; which will require character-building sacrifice and which will encourage soul-killing dependency; which will make us safer and which will add fuel to the ISIS fire; which will carry the American banner proudly and which will grovel and plead that we be forgiven for being the greatest country this world has ever known.

Whichever side of the political continuum you pick, whichever candidate you decide is best-suited to lead our country forward in these turbulent times, choose wisely; when we go over those rapids, there's no getting out of the boat.

American Exceptionalism

Let's start with how the candidates feel about America. Do they believe in American exceptionalism? Or do they think we are exceptional to ourselves the way the Greeks are exceptional to themselves and the Brazilians to themselves. Our Founding Fathers were inspired to create an absolutely brilliant form of government that has made us the most powerful, the *most prosperous, and the most freedom-drenched nation that has ever existed anytime, anywhere* in human history.

That. Is. Exceptional. We need a president who knows that and who wears it proudly.

The Constitution and the Rule of Law

Do the candidates recognize what a brilliant—again brilliant—document the Constitution is? We are unique in that we view our rights as derived from God. Life, liberty, and the pursuit of happiness are God-given and cannot be taken away by Man. Our Constitution embodies that view by enshrining and protecting those rights.

Will the candidates work within the constraints of the Constitution to change laws? Or will it be a pen and a phone on a Tuesday afternoon? The Constitution is the only thing standing between us and anarchy, and we need a president—constitutional scholar or not—who understands its constraints and agrees to subject him- or herself to them.

The Constitution is the only thing standing between us and anarchy, and we need a president—constitutional scholar or not—who understands its constraints and agrees to subject him- or herself to them.

Free Speech and Microaggressions

Do the candidates believe that free speech is a right afforded to all or a privilege granted to only those individuals in marginalized groups? A recent piece[3] in The New Yorker declared, "The freedom to offend the powerful is not equivalent to the freedom to bully the relatively disempowered." No? Who decides the consequences for whom if speech is not free to all? That prerogative can change like the wind and is precisely why we have a First Amendment. And it is why we need a president who defends to the death the right of every citizen to utter abhorrent speech.

Parents' Relationship to Their Children

Where do the candidates draw the line between the power parents have to raise their children according to their values and the power the government has to interfere with that relationship? Take a 14-year-old girl who becomes pregnant. Do the candidates think she should be able to get an abortion without her parents ever knowing? That's the litmus test right there.

The War on Women

Do the candidates play on our fears about affordable birth control, legal abortion, and fairness in pay between men and women? Do they rile us up and then promise to rescue us from this "war on women?" Don't fall for it. Roe v. Wade isn't going anywhere no matter who is elected; birth control is cheap and covered by Obamacare; and the gender pay gap is about choices in education and occupational field, job demands, and number of hours worked over the span of a career.

---

3 Jelani Cobb, "Free speech and the race diversion," *The New Yorker*, November 10, 2015, http://www.newyorker.com/news/news-desk/race-and-the-free-speech-diversion.

The war on women is a ginned up conflagration of fear, victimhood, and self-righteousness. Don't let manipulated emotion override cool evaluation of legitimate issues like ISIS and illegal immigration.

Don't let manipulated emotion override cool evaluation of legitimate issues like ISIS and illegal immigration.

Terrorism—the ISIS Kind

Evaluate the candidates on their willingness to tell the truth about fundamentalist Islamic jihadi terrorism. If a candidate calls Ft. Hood or San Bernardino "workplace violence," run for the hills. Dr. Phil says, "You can't fix what you don't acknowledge," and I couldn't agree more. We don't stop ISIS terrorists with workplace diversity training.

We don't stop ISIS terrorists with workplace diversity training.

Foreign Policy: Do We Bomb Innocent Civilians or Not?

Do the candidates believe we have a right to survive as a culture and to maintain our safety and way of life by any means necessary? This is the most difficult question because we are talking about the willingness—when absolutely necessary—to sacrifice the lives of innocent people in order to protect our own. If we are the evil nation President Obama apologized for around the world, we don't deserve to exist. If instead we are truly exceptional and an asset to the rest of the world, we have a duty to exist.

Illegal Immigration

Evaluate the candidates on two aspects: their focus and their plan. Are they willing to use the words "illegal immigration?" Are they willing to acknowledge what a catastrophe illegal immigration is for our country? Or do they dance around it because they might hurt the feelings of people who might feel marginalized? They are marginalized. That's why it's called "living in the shadows." If we can't speak the truth about that, we have a bigger problem than our border.

Are they willing to acknowledge what a catastrophe illegal immigration is for our country? If we can't speak the truth about that, we have a bigger problem than our border.

Small Business Regulation

How will the candidates treat small business? Women start the majority of small businesses in this country, and the harder it is to start a business, the harder it is for women to provide for their families and achieve the work-life balance they seek. We need a president who is willing to get in there and slash and burn through all the burdensome, often ludicrous, government regulation, and loosen its stranglehold on entrepreneurship.

Foreign Policy

We are the most powerful and influential country on earth. We need a president who is willing to use that power and influence to further our interests in the world. We're allowed to act in our own self-interest; it's not evil. It's good for us when we work in our best interest, and it's good for our allies. We're the good guys. Let's go get 'em.

**We're allowed to act in our own self-interest;
we're the good guys.**

Fiscal Responsibility

This is a no-brainer. The government has no money of its own; the only money it has to spend is the money it takes from me, and you, and every other taxpayer. Will the candidates use our money wisely, make hard choices now that require immediate sacrifice to right our economic shipwreck? Or will the candidates cook the books to spend the money they want to today, content to let somebody else pay the price down the road? Well, who is it that's going to pay the price? It's our children and grandchildren. We need a president who puts the well-being of America and of our descendants above their own political power today.

My personal values and vision are unabashedly pro-America. This book is unabashedly pro-America. I hope you find it helpful in clarifying your own values and vision.

Donna Carol Voss
Kaysville, Utah
February 6, 2016

AMERICAN EXCEPTIONALISM

Does the candidate understand how exceptional we truly are?

The people in every society since the dawn of time have been poor. Until America.

The people in every society since the dawn of time have been at the mercy of rulers and governments. Until America.

The people in every society since the dawn of time have been trapped in the social class to which they were born. Until America.

If that is not the definition of exceptional, what is?

Shortly after taking office in 2009, during a press conference at the NATO Summit in Strasbourg France, President Obama said Americans weren't exceptional in thinking we were exceptional. "I believe in American exceptionalism, just as I suspect that the Brits believe in British exceptionalism and the Greeks believe in Greek exceptionalism."

Kind of like telling a group of young people that each one of them is special; if they're all special, how can anyone be special? If we're all exceptional, how can any country be exceptional?

Then, doubling back on himself in his signature move, the president stated that "our belief in free speech and equality … [is] exceptional."

So, are we exceptionally exceptional or not? Ladies and gentlemen, I give you…the Founders and the separation of powers.

The Founders AKA the Founding Fathers

I dare say it—our country was founded by men. Rich, white, slave-owning men. Oh well. Martin Luther King and John F. Kennedy were womanizers, but it didn't lessen their contribution to society. Acknowledging that the Founders fail today's politically correct standards by a mile, let's consider who they were, and how they came to establish an absolutely brilliant form of government.

Acknowledging that the Founders fail today's politically correct standards by a mile, let's consider who they were, and how they came to establish an absolutely brilliant form of government.

Why is it so important for some people to contend, nay, insist, that not all the Founding Fathers were Christian? So what? Not a one of them was atheist; not a one of them thought the human race was here with no connection to the Divine. The divine spark that animated each man individually also inspired them as a group to reach beyond the limits of human intellect, organization, and communication (as in writing; as in Thomas Jefferson; as in the Declaration of Independence). The result was—wait for it—exceptional.

We were the first government in history to declare—boldly—that our rights come from God and not the king. Life, liberty, and the pursuit of happiness were seen as inalienable rights (some people say "unalienable," but I personally checked the Jefferson Memorial, and it says "inalienable"). They were inalienable because they could not be taken away or given away. Rights that could not be changed at the political whim of a ruler were a revolutionary idea. Given by God, they exist outside of society and bring all people to a level playing field before Him.

> **We were the first government in history to declare—boldly—that our rights come from God and not the king. Rights that could not be changed at the political whim of a ruler were a revolutionary idea. Given by God, they exist outside of society and bring all people to a level playing field before Him.**

The Three-Fifths Compromise

Okay, the three-fifths thing. It sounds outrageous at first blush; it isn't. During the Constitutional Convention in 1787, it was agreed that a slave would be counted as three-fifths of a free man for the purpose of legislative representation. A state's total population dictated how much legislative representation the state would receive in the form of congressional seats and electoral votes, i.e., the greater the population, the greater the number of seats in the House of Representative, just as it is today.

Delegates fought bitterly over the number of seats and votes to be apportioned between northern and southern states. Delegates opposed to slavery lobbied that only free men be counted in the numbers in order to reduce the legislative power of the South; delegates in favor of slavery lobbied against the idea, wanting slaves to count in their actual numbers, which would give their state more representation in Congress.

And so the Three-Fifths Compromise was born.

The Three-Fifths Compromise, rather than diminishing the human value of blacks as opposed to whites instead diminished the power of Southern states to enslave blacks. Isn't that a good thing?

Even counting slaves as only 3/5 of a person, the Southern states still received a third more seats in the House and a third more electoral votes than if the slaves had been ignored; can you imagine how great the power imbalance would have been had slaves been counted exactly the same as free men? The three-fifths rule, properly understood, was a tool to eventually defeat slavery. The three-fifths compromise, properly understood, is a non-starter.

All Men Are Created Equal

Not true! cry the uninformed masses. When our country was founded, blacks were enslaved and had no rights; women could neither vote nor own property—how is that equal? But merely the vision of equality between blacks and whites, between men and women was radical; no other government went so far as to even suggest it, let alone put it in writing. Our founders envisioned and committed to the ideal long before it was possible in society.

Is it not brilliant to apprehend a vision long before the fact of its accomplishment is even on the horizon? For many of us, that brilliance reveals the hand of our Creator in the events of our founding. If a Creator is not your thing, it makes the Founding Fathers even more brilliant to have come up with this on their own, no?

Separation of Powers

You can be forgiven if you have no idea what I'm talking about, because at this point, the separation is theoretical. Plus, if you've been through the public school system, you were too busy learning about climate change and the contributions of LGBT citizens to learn how the government actually works. Is supposed to work. Did work for a long time.

If you've been through the public school system, you were too busy learning about climate change and the contributions of LGBT citizens to learn how the government actually works. Is supposed to work. Did work for a long time.

Think of the separation of powers as an ingenious rock-paper-scissors game played with the Legislative, the Judicial, and the Executive Branches of government. (That's Congress, the Supreme Court, and the president for those of you Keeping Up with the Kardashians.) In the rock-paper-scissors game, scissors cut paper, paper covers rock, and rock breaks scissors. Each element is both stronger than and subject to another element. That makes it, like, fair.

In the separation of powers, each branch of government is both stronger than and subject to another branch of government. Using a system of checks and balances—rock, paper, scissors—no branch is able to gain so much power over the others that we end up with a tyrannical government.

**In the separation of powers, each branch of government is
both stronger than and subject to another branch of government. Using a system of checks and balances, no branch is
able to gain so much power over the others that we end up
with a tyrannical government.**

In theory, the president has to work through Congress to pass laws
but can veto any bill that comes to the presidential desk. (I'm dying to
make a crack about a phone and a pen on a Tuesday afternoon, but it
would mess up my flow.) The president is required to obtain the approval
of Congress before declaring war.

Again, in theory—almost unimaginable theory—the Supreme Court
interprets the laws passed by Congress in light of our Constitution and
is immune to social pressure. It has the power to declare laws unconstitutional and therefore void. Through Congress, Supreme Court justices
can be impeached (charged with misconduct and potentially removed
from office, for those of you on season six of the Walking Dead).

Congress has the power to tax and spend, control the budget, confirm
judges, and ratify treaties. It can override a presidential veto with a
two-thirds majority in both the House of Representatives and the Senate.
The president can mandate that either house or both houses be called
into Emergency Session, and neither the House nor the Senate has power
to intervene in presidential pardons.

Separation of powers—could a more perfect system be designed? Not
that it operates perfectly, but it is a shining beacon of the genius inherent
in our founding.Our system of government has made us the freest, most

powerful, most prosperous nation that has ever existed in human history, or that exists on the earth at this time.

Separation of powers—could a more perfect system be designed? Not that it operates perfectly, but it is a shining beacon of the genius inherent in our founding.

That, my fellow Americans, is exceptionally exceptional. We need a president who knows that and wears it proudly.

THE CONSTITUTION AND THE RULE OF LAW

Does the candidate recognize what an absolutely brilliant document we have for running our country?

This area naturally follows on from American Exceptionalism because the U.S. Constitution is the most remarkable—remarkable—document ever framed by Man. We need a president who has a healthy respect and sense of awe for the document and is willing to work within its constraints to effect changes in the law. Clearly this is a better place for my crack about a phone and a pen on a Tuesday afternoon.

The U.S. Constitution is the most remarkable—remarkable—document ever framed by Man. We need a president who has a healthy respect and sense of awe for the document and is willing to work within its constraints to effect changes in the law.

As I laid out in the last chapter, our government operates as an ingenious rock-paper-scissors game; paper covers rock, scissors cut paper, and rock breaks scissors. The Constitution checks and balances the president's power to change laws; or, it covers, cuts, or breaks personal whim, however you prefer to frame it.

What would happen if rock suddenly started sitting on paper, or paper started binding scissors, or scissors started pulverizing rock? We would have an entirely different game. What happens when the president ignores the Constitution—uses a pen and a phone on a Tuesday afternoon? We have an entirely different system that no longer enshrines and protects our freedoms.

As Americans, and uniquely as Americans, we have a Constitutional right to be free from tyranny, i.e., cruel and oppressive government or rule. "Cruel and oppressive" does not mean the voluntary suffering that comes when we don't get the laws we want changed or enacted. Sorry, but that's just life.

"Cruel and oppressive" means the repudiation of basic human rights established so clearly in the U.S. with the birth of our country. The opposite—imposing rights that were never established—is also cruel and oppressive in that it stacks the deck in favor of the wily opponent.

Stacking the deck is an "ends justify the means" philosophy; They the People who want certain laws enacted or changed know better than you and me what is right, so they try to make it happen at all costs, in which case the Constitution carries as much weight as a wet mosquito.

Think of the Constitution as a great aircraft carrier defining and protecting our path. A carrier can be made to alter its path or come to a complete stop, but it requires gargantuan effort and teamwork. The Constitution is designed to be just as difficult to alter, requiring a two-thirds majority in both houses of Congress to do so.

Think of the Constitution as a great aircraft carrier defining and protecting our path. A carrier can be made to alter its path or come to a complete stop, but it requires gargantuan effort and teamwork. The Constitution is designed to be just as difficult to alter, requiring a two-thirds majority in both houses of Congress to do so.

We have altered it many times, and will alter it again for the right reason. The First Amendment defined the essence of our country; the Second Amendment defined the character of our country; and the Nineteenth Amendment justified the ideals of our country. (If you don't know what the 19th Amendment brought about, you must forever tear up your feminism card. We are, however, accepting recovering feminists over at 21st Century Women[4].)

Amendments are powerful in shaping our lives and should be messed with only when necessary. We can change our minds about amendments we've passed and remove them again, but they shape our lives powerfully while they exist. The Eighteenth Amendment that was meant to dry us out like a church house was reversed by the Twenty-first Amendment that bowed to reality. Americans. Like. To. Drink. In the nominally dry years between amendments (1920-1933), great American fortunes were made through bootlegging, and NASCAR was born in its earliest form of souped up cars to escape the Law.

---

4   The website for 21st Century Women; WeAre21stCenturyWomen.com

"Messed with only when necessary" implies using the legally approved means for doing so. The last thing we need is a rodeo president who shoots from the hip; when that happens, We the People lose. Four examples in contemporary society illustrate the way a president can skirt the Constitution, either by ignoring it or by fundamentally transforming it into something it was never meant to be.

The last thing we need is a rodeo president who shoots from the hip.

Gun Control

The right to own and use a gun is fairly important to Americans. So much so that we dedicated a whole amendment to it, the Second: "A well regulated Militia, being necessary to the security of a free State, the right of the people to keep and bear Arms, shall not be infringed."

Succinct, to the point, and powerful.

In our longish history, the Supreme Court has at times interpreted the language as an individual right and at other times as a collective right. The difference between the two interpretations is profound—fundamentally a life or death issue.

Under an individual right interpretation, you and I can possess a gun, and Congress is prohibited from restricting r excessively regulating our use. We the People have the power to protect ourselves and our families, and to defend our homes. If we should happen to attend the midnight premiere of Batman on the day it opens, we are not hapless helpless victims if a crazy redhead uses the theater for target practice. (Unless we're in a politically-contrived, gun-free zone, in which case we're toast.)

Under a collective right interpretation, Congress can regulate and restrict our personal gun use at will but is prohibited from restricting or excessively regulating the state's use. You and I have no power to protect ourselves and our families, or to defend our homes. If a burglar breaks into our home and threatens to hurt our children, the only thing we can do is hope to make a 911 call and pray that the police get there in time. We are hapless and helpless, just the way the burglar wants us.

To be law-abiding citizens, which most of us are, we have to follow the gun laws as they are currently interpreted by the Court. In 1939, the Court ruled in United States v. Miller[5] that the Second Amendment was framed to ensure the effectiveness of our military and not as a guarantee of individual gun ownership. Congress was then permitted to regulate personal firearms—the dreaded sawed-off shotgun for instance—if they bore no reasonable relationship to maintaining an efficient militia.

Seventy years later in 2008, the pendulum swung to the individual right interpretation when the Court ruled in District of Columbia v. Heller[6] that handgun bans were unconstitutional. If you subsequently wanted a gun in Washington D.C., Congress could no longer prohibit you from getting a gun in Washington D.C. Congress could still, the Court decided, severely restrict access to personal firearms by criminals and the mentally ill. Our unfortunate friend the sawed-off shotgun was also excluded from the party since law-abiding citizens cannot use sawed-off shotguns for any law abiding purpose.

---

5   United States v. Miller, 307 U.S. 174 (1939).

6   District of Columbia v. Heller, 554 U.S. 570, (2008).

We need a president who follows the gun laws as currently interpreted by the Supreme Court. As much as the president may abhor guns and however vigorously he or she fights to change the laws, he or she must submit to defeat if unsuccessful.

We do not want a president who, if defeated coming through the front door (i.e., working within the constraints of the Constitution), finds a back door, like, I don't know, buying up all the ammunition. So guns are still legal, but ammunition to use them is unavailable or exorbitantly expensive. Sound familiar?

We do not want a president who, if defeated coming through the front door (i.e., working within the constraints of the Constitution), finds a back door.

Gay Marriage

No matter who we are, the topic of gay marriage pings our fundamental personal values, and often not in a serene way. The history of its affirmation by the Supreme Court is full of dramatic twists and turns, but I'll save you some time with the cliff notes.

God created the heavens and the earth, and gave as the first commandment to Adam and Eve that they should multiply and replenish the earth. Sometime thereafter, He communicated to His children that homosexual acts were sinful (some religions explain this as the natural follow-on to the first commandment, in that homosexual acts cannot by definition lead to multiplying and replenishing the earth). God felt so strongly about this prohibition that He repeated it with emphasis. Judeo-Christian cultures followed that edict by criminalizing sexual behavior between men. (There was also sexual behavior between women, but they knew how to keep it under wraps. Plus, nobody cared what women did. Sorry, but it's true.)

Fast forward to modern times where most Judeo-Christian countries no longer criminalize the behavior. After decriminalization, successive social waves advanced most of us beyond beating, ostracizing, disapproving, or judging, and ultimately brought us to tolerating and/or embracing homosexuality depending on your point of view.

Cue scene.

External – California – Eve of Proposition 8

Mini Armageddon begins, and all hell breaks loose between good guys, bad guys, and everyone in-between. First one side wins, then the other, then back to the first, then back to the other. Rinse. Repeat.

When the smoke clears, 52 percent of people in the state of California have voted to amend the state constitution to define marriage between one man and one woman. (Those of you who like logic puzzles, there's a doozy here. If voters had to amend the constitution to codify 3000 years of human practice, it means that marriage was not established as a right when the state constitution was initially framed. Ditto the United States Constitution, but we're getting ahead of ourselves.)

Drumroll please.

Once citizens of the state had passed Prop 8, public officials were required to defend the law. They. Did. Not. (Note that public officials elected to uphold the laws of the state declined to uphold a law they didn't like. Is that rejecting the constraints of the state constitution or what?)

Trust me when I say the twists and turns got even more dramatic. After a whole lot of legal mumbo jumbo, voters woke up one bright and sunny California morning to find that their wishes were null and void[7].

Gay marriage could go forward in California.

From there it was a locomotive picking up speed until the issue reached the United States Supreme Court in 2015. Same kind of dance where the U.S. Constitution grants no right of marriage to the people, but the Justices managed to make gay marriage a *de facto* right anyhow (*de facto* as in "give us your lunch money").

Sanctuary Cities

On June 4, 2007, New Haven, CT was the first city in the country to declare itself[8] above federal immigration law. As of October, 2015, 339 additional American cities[9] likewise had declared their intention to flout our laws. This particular kind of defiance may include formal policies that prevent state employees from reporting the presence of illegal aliens; and informal practices such as a city council adopting a resolution in opposition to the enforcement of U.S. immigration laws. (Didn't we all learn in high school that federal law trumps state law when federal law is more restrictive?) At any point, the Obama administration could have and still could prosecute states for lawlessness. Instead, Mr. Obama blocked a bill intended to strip sanctuary cities of federal funds, his veto in line with Democrats who called the GOP bill "vile legislation." Those opposed to the bill claimed it was "designed to demonize immigrants and spread the myth

---

7 Hollingsworth v. Perry, 570 U.S. ___, (2013).

8 "The original list of sanctuary cities, USA," last modified December 12, 2015, accessed January 30, 2016, http://www.ojjpac.org/sanctuary.asp.

9 Stephen Dinan, "Number of sanctuary cities grows to 340; thousands of illegals released to commit new crimes," Washington Times, October 8, 2015, http://www.washingtontimes.com/news/2015/oct/8/number-of-sanctuary-cities-grows-to-340-thousands-/.

that they are criminals and threats to the public." Because of personal whim, the leader of our country declines to hold states accountable to the Constitution.

Because of personal whim, the leader of our country declines to hold states accountable to the Constitution.

Legalization of Marijuana

Federal law classifies marijuana as a Schedule I substance, which means it has a high potential for abuse and dependency. Accordingly, it is a federal crime to possess, cultivate, or use marijuana; violators are subject to fines, prison time, or both. Nonetheless, four states—Alaska, Colorado, Washington, and Oregon—have legalized the use of recreational marijuana[10], i.e., no penalty. In what universe do states have the option of violating federal law? In the troubling universe where a president declines to respond.

How would the president's administration resolve a conflict between state and federal law? If I rent my house, and my tenant both grows marijuana and trashes my house (not suggesting a connection), which law do I follow? State law allows me to sue for destruction of my property, but federal law says the government could potentially seize my home for my failure to prevent drug-related illegal activity on the premises. Crazy.

---

10   Sam Stebbins, Thomas C. Frohlich, and Michael B. Sauter, "The next 11 states to legalize marijuana," *24/7 Wall Street*, August 8, 2015, http://247wallst.com/special-report/2015/08/12/the-next-11-states-to-legalize-marijuana/.

As more and more power is taken away from the people of our country and concentrated in the hands of a few Robed Ones —and with the added arbitrariness of a president who picks and chooses which laws to enforce—we cease to be the greatest country on earth. If a handful of people can decide for the rest of us how our country will be, we might as well live in Venezuela.

As more and more power is taken away from the people of our country and concentrated in the hands of a few Robed Ones —and with the added arbitrariness of a president who picks and chooses which laws to enforce—we cease to be the greatest country on earth. If a handful of people can decide for the rest of us how our country will be, we might as well live in Venezuela.

The United States Constitution is the only thing that stands between us and a state of anarchy where only the elites have power. We need a president who believes in "We the people, by the people, and for the people" even if the people have a politically incorrect mind of our own. A president who, rather than laying claim to being a constitutional scholar, actually understands and agrees to subject him or herself to the rule of law. A president who takes the oath of office seriously and takes it on a Bible, if only out of respect to our Judeo-Christian heritage. It is that heritage that created the presidential office requiring said oath, and the process by which said office is attained. It deserves a shout-out.

We need a president who believes in "We the people, by the people, and for the people" even if the people have a politically incorrect mind of our own.

FREE SPEECH AND MICROAGGRESSIONS

Does the candidate understand that the purpose of our First Amendment is to protect the most odious of speech; believe that Americans have a right to think for ourselves; and trust that we are capable of considering other points of view without having a nervous breakdown?

F ree speech is the canary in the coal mine; when it goes, we're done for. Microaggressions are the cancer of a free society; when they take over, we're reduced to politically correct verbal automatons. Please allow Psychology Today to define microaggressions:

> *"Everyday verbal, nonverbal, and environmental slights, snubs, or insults, whether intentional or unintentional, which communicate hostile, derogatory, or negative messages to target persons based solely upon their marginalized group membership."*

Next, please allow Wikipedia to define a related term—intersectionality[11]—without which microaggressions make it only halfway around the track:

> *"Intersectionality holds that the classical conceptualizations of oppression within society, such as racism, sexism, classism, ableism, biphobia, homopobia, transphobia and belief-based bigotry, do not act independently of one another. Instead, these forms of oppression interrelate, creating a system of oppression that reflects the "intersection" of multiple forms of discrimination."*

Free Speech

Free speech. The essence of America. Not so much anymore.

There are still those of us who revere it as near sacred, but we are rapidly being overwhelmed by those who think it is a privilege for only the few—and not the few we normally refer to as privileged. No, in this case, free speech is free for only the marginalized.

Free speech. The essence of America. Not so much anymore.

The points of view line up as follows: On the right side of the heavyweight boxing ring, we have Mr. USA. (And for all the feminists right now who are offended that I've made him male, get over it. No one wants to imagine sweaty, beefy women duking it out in a boxing ring. That's just wrong.)

---

11   *Wikipedia*, s.v. "Intersectionality," accessed December 20, 2015, https://en.wikipedia.org/wiki/Intersectionality.

On the left side of the ring, we have Mr. Fundamental Transformation, or Mr. FT for short.

Mr. USA has trained diligently for the match; plenty of sleep, fresh veggies, protein, and daily workouts in the gym. Mr. FT, on the other hand, was bullied as a child, so he feels entitled to take a few shortcuts; late nights with the ladies, Krispy Kremes and diet Coke, and daily workouts with the remote control.

The bell rings, and before the first punch is thrown, Mr. FT calls a flag on the play (or whatever the equivalent is in boxing.) "It's not fair," he cries. "Mr. USA has an advantage over me because he wasn't bullied as a child. All his life he's had the privilege of a bully-free childhood. That makes him evil. If he doesn't acknowledge his evil privilege, it's just more proof of his evilness. I demand advantages for myself to level the playing field."

The referee is thrown off guard by this bold move to change the rules of the game, and doesn't react immediately. Inside his head, he thinks, "*Is this guy for real? A boxing match is a boxing match. The same rules apply to everyone, and if you've had more challenges than the other guy, oh well, that's life. In fact, you're probably stronger than the other guy for having to overcome them.*"

Mr. FT, observing the ref's hesitation, presses forward. "Mr. USA needs to fight with one hand tied behind his back to make it fair!"

The ref and Mr. USA gape open-mouthed at Mr. FT. It's a joke, right? The rules of boxing are well-established; if both fighters are not held to the same rules, it's not boxing anymore.

Then Mr. FT brings it home with, "You two are bullies! If you don't give me what I want, I'm going to make your lives a living hell. I can get you fired, publish your home addresses, start a smear campaign on social media, and have this boxing match outlawed."

And so it is with free speech in America. One side is demanding that the rules of the game be changed to give them the advantage, which advantage they insist is merely a reversing of longstanding advantage to the other side. White privilege is a fact, they say, no matter what socio-economic category whites find themselves in; any whites who deny their privilege are only proving how privileged (read evil) they are.

Because of white privilege, whites are not allowed to say anything that upsets non-whites, and, just for good measure, Christians are not allowed to say anything that upsets non-Christians. If white Christians dare argue that they have every right to voice their opinion, they are accused of "erasing minority experience." Heaven help the whites if they're affluent, professionally successful, and sincere in their beliefs; a deadly combination because those folks tend to play by the rules. And the whole point of invoking white privilege is to change the rules of the game.

The whole point of invoking white privilege is to change the rules of the game. To change the rules of the game, you have to change the hearts and minds of the people.

To change the rules of the game, you have to change the hearts and minds of the people. Where does one get the most bang for one's buck in changing hearts and minds? As ISIS can tell you, it's on social media, Twitter and Facebook in particular. Facebook tends to be more of a rallying point while Twitter serves as the Great Divide.

Twitter is one of the few places left in life where people can still encounter differing opinions in a relatively IED-free environment. If the convo heats up, there's something called "Block," which lets you banish your enemy forever. If you want to know anything about free speech, spend ten minutes on Twitter following people from both the right and the left.

A recent exchange between myself and a man who works for an LGBT publication says it all. He posted an article from the New Yorker called "Race and the Free-Speech Diversion"[12] with the comment, *Great perspective on how those who insist on the "free speech" right to defend are just propping up white privilege.*

Intrigued by the idea that "insisting" on "free speech" was somehow a negative, I read the article. One sentence stood out to me: *"Freedom to offend the powerful is not equivalent to freedom to bully the relatively disempowered."* I responded *"Actually, it is."* And off to the races we went:

Him: All too easy to say when you're part of the powerful and can't speak to the experience of daily disempowerment.

Me: Easy to say doesn't make it any less true.

Him: All too true that you're blinded and spoiled by your own privileges.

Me: If we can't agree that free speech is a right granted to all and not a privilege enjoyed by a few, what common ground is there?

Him: I didn't say anybody's speech wasn't free. But free speech doesn't mean consequence-free speech.

Me: But who decides what consequences and for whom? That prerogative can change with the wind & is precisely why we have a 1st Amend.

Him: I'm not talking legal consequences, I'm talking public accountability. It's free speech on all sides.

---

12 Jelani Cobb, "Free speech and the race diversion," *The New Yorker*, November 10, 2015, http://www.newyorker.com/news/news-desk/race-and-the-free-speech-diversion.

Me: What's the difference? Both are negative consequences for free speech, which makes it, um, not free.

Him: When you spew or defend prejudice, the speech that calls you out is just as free.

Me: Speech, absolutely. A screaming banshee in your face with no remorse who calls for you losing your job, no.

Him: Who are you thinking of?

Me: Watch recent video from Black Lives Matter or the Safe Space movement. Although to be fair, some have expressed remorse.

Him: What kind of speech protections do you believe are wavering?

Me: The ability to express politically incorrect views without losing your job or being skewered in social media.

Me: The right for your public speech to be just as free as those you abhor is the whole point of the 1st Amend.

Him: You're assuming some sort of legal determination or change of law. I just don't understand your umbrage.

Me: Nothing formal, just mob rule that hurts people's livelihood is what I notice.

Him: Mob rule? If a whole bunch of people are telling you you're bigoted … could just be that they're right.

Me: And you may be right. That's why it's so important to protect all speech. We have the freedom to be bigots. #GoUSA

Him: Sure, but that doesn't mean you don't face consequences. You are accountable for your speech, free as it may be.

Me: Absolutely. But accountable to whom? Coddled students who don't want hurt feelings? That's mob rule not accountability.

It would be wrong of me to imply that I had the last word on the matter. But for the purposes of illustration, I've conveyed enough of our exchange. The bottom line is that some of us no longer uphold the right of free speech for all as a divinely inspired rule, a rule that was established during the birth of our country and that distinguishes us from virtually all other countries past and present.

Others among us view the "divinely inspired" notion with suspicion if not downright hostility. Because the Bill of Rights was framed by white, affluent, slave-owning men, several of whom were Christian, the First Amendment is regarded by suspicious hostiles as unenforceable. At least unenforceable as written, intended, and practiced until "intersectional politics" were born.

Because the Bill of Rights was framed by white, affluent, slave-owning men, several of whom were Christian, the First Amendment is regarded by suspicious hostiles as unenforceable. At least unenforceable as written, intended, and practiced until "intersectional politics" were born.

We need a president with the intellectual clarity to see our Founders through the lens of their contemporary society and not our own. How many of us used words in the past ("gay," "oriental," "handi-capped," "colored," "retarded") that today are viewed in a completely different light and abandoned by overall consensus for more culturally sensitive words? (Although, some, like my mother who was born in 1927, forever mourned the loss of "gay" as "merry, happy, and light.")

We didn't use those words because we were evil; we used them because those were the words that were used back then. Our Bill of Rights isn't evil because it was framed by white, male, mostly Christian, slave-owning men; it was framed by them because those were the folks who had the power back then. Are we really going to throw out the baby with the bathwater?

We need a president who honors the Bill of Rights as written, intended, and practiced until "intersectional politics" were born.

We need a president with the intellectual clarity to see our Founders through the lens of their contemporary society and not our own.

Microaggressions

Microaggressions are a fascinating corruption of free speech; they also poison Halloween costumes, Christmas pageants, and the biologically-driven, imminently pleasurable practice of flirting. Remember, in the quest for the Holy Grail of undisturbed psyches, microaggressions are defined as

*"Everyday verbal, nonverbal, and environmental slights, snubs, or insults, whether intentional or unintentional, which communicate hostile, derogatory, or negative messages to target persons **based solely upon** their marginalized group membership."*

I've highlighted the operative words of the definition—"based solely upon"—because they are the magic beans that render any speech offensive to anyone at any time who just knows in their heart that it is "based solely upon" their membership in a marginalized group.

Microaggressions are a fascinating corruption of free speech.

And what is the measure of the speaker's intent? The objective evidence that would reveal the attitude behind the speech? Exactly. There is none. Until we enter the phase of human development where we can read each other's minds, our thoughts remain our own and not subject to scrutiny by the Thought Police.

Not to mention that most of us suffer a handful of "slights, snubs, or insults, whether intentional or unintentional, which communicate hostile, derogatory, or negative messages" before lunch every day. The driver who cuts you off; the co-worker who shoots a meaningful glance at another co-worker when you enter the room; the boss who fails to give you credit for the success of the project; the neighbor who wantonly blocks your driveway; your own children, even, who call you "mean" and say, "I hate you."

The worst thing about accusations of microaggressions is that they bring normally intelligent, confident, open-minded people to their knees in a wash of pleading, cajoling, and capitulation. University presidents and chancellors are forced out of careers; businesses are pressured to apologize to—and often give money to—groups that accuse them of, well, just about anything they feel like. And the biggest stick of all, the nuclear option that stops just about anyone in their tracks: being called a "racist." "Hateful" and "bigot" are pretty powerful, too.

The worst thing about accusations of microaggressions is that they bring normally intelligent, confident, open-minded people to their knees in a wash of pleading, cajoling, and capitulation.

Ironically, it's often the nicest, most fair-minded people who compromise their values, their speech, and their behavior to avoid such labels. The slippery slope result is that the sharks smell blood in the water and go, go, go. Twitter is instructive yet again. My LGBT debate partner and I went a few rounds on microaggression as well.

Him: What's really happening in higher ed is a new intellectual standard for respecting others. It's unsurprisingly NOT conservative.

Me: That's funny. Treating people like they're too fragile to handle conflict & diff POVs doesn't sound like respect to me.

Him: When you use the word "fragile," you're blaming the victim for not enduring intolerance. It's disgusting.

Me: Most people throughout history have endured intolerance to their great moral development. I'm actually believing in the victim.

Him: But you're not helping relieve them of the burden of being a victim. What does that say about you?

Me: Pressure tempers steel and turns carbon to diamond. Discrimination is illegal so the burden now is words. They can handle words.

Him: Wow! You're actually admitting that you don't care about reducing hate beyond ending discrimination. How sad. And foolish.

Me: Yes. I'm admitting that eradicating hate is a pipe dream. Pursuing the impossible does, however, keep lots of folks employed.

Him: Wow. Well, don't ever try to call yourself an ally again.

Me: That's where we disagree. An ally gives it to you straight, supports your efforts, and cheers your successes. I'm betting on me.

We need a president who cuts off the notion of microaggression before it can put on its pants. We need a president who respects all citizens enough to require a little hardiness of them. We need a president who reinforces the very mechanism of American ingenuity and prosperity: overcoming obstacles.

We need a president who cuts off the notion of microaggression before it can put on its pants. We need a president who respects all citizens enough to require a little hardiness of them.

PARENTS' RELATIONSHIP TO THEIR CHILDREN

Will the candidate support parents in raising their children as they see fit, or will government be allowed to undermine and interfere with parents' politically incorrect values?

If there is a more fundamental relationship in society than parent to child, I don't know what it is. More than any other impact on our lives, the relationship we have with our parents influences us the most deeply and the most permanently. For the most part, no one loves a child like his parents (again, feminists, get over it), and no one is more invested in a child's decency, well-being, happiness, and success.

If there is a more fundamental relationship in society than parent to child, I don't know what it is.

The variety of ways a child's parents can structure their relationship—or not—is secondary to the inviolate bond between parent and child. As can be seen from the Twitter exchanges in Chapter Two, different people often have very different views of the same issue.

Going out on a limb, I assume that my LGBT debate partner will teach his children that gay marriage is both a civil right and a beautiful thing. I, on the other hand, will teach my children a biblically-based view of the sacredness of marriage between one man and one woman.

Whatever he and I think of each other or our respective points of view, neither of us would presume to break down the other's door and hijack the home's value system. So why should the government be able to do so?

I always go back to the inspired genius of our Founders. The principle of limited government rescued us from tyranny and empowered our prosperity. The Founders set up a federal government[13] to "establish Justice, insure domestic Tranquility, provide for the common defence, promote the general Welfare, and secure the Blessings of Liberty to ourselves and our Posterity." At the risk of insulting all but the Honey Boo Boo fans, let me explain that the federal government is parent to all state governments; it is concerned with only the issues that affect the entire family/nation and has the last word in any disagreement. (Theoretically. See chapter 2.)

At the risk of insulting all but the Honey Boo Boo fans, let me explain that the federal government is parent to all state governments; it is concerned with only the issues that affect the entire family/nation and has the last word in any disagreement.

---

13   U.S. Constitution, preamble, http://www.archives.gov/exhibits/charters/constitution_transcript.html.

As all healthy children thrive with maximum effective independence from their parents, states thrive with maximum effective independence from the federal government. We the parents thrive with as little interference from either government as possible. We tolerate the state's interference to protect children from neglect and abuse, and to require that they receive a certain amount of education. Sounds straightforward, no? No.

As all healthy children thrive with maximum effective independence from their parents, states thrive with maximum effective independence from the federal government.

Most of us agree on the obvious examples of abuse and neglect—putting out cigarettes on little bodies, depriving them of food, violating their innocence—and also on education minimums—teaching our children to read and write. After that, abuse, neglect, and education are in the eye of the beholder.

When parents have power and authority to control their children's behavior and education, the relationship between parents and children is strengthened. When government has power and authority to usurp parents' control of their children's behavior and education, the relationship between parents and children is injured.

When parents have power and authority to control their children's behavior and education, the relationship between parents and children is strengthened.

Conservative parents, at least those who send their children to public school, overwhelmingly view education as a body of knowledge and practice their children will need to function effectively in life: science, math, geology, language arts, etc. Conservative parents reserve for themselves the prerogative of teaching their children about social issues, especially sexual mores.

Liberal parents, conversely, overwhelmingly view education as an opportunity to shape the minds of future citizens toward liberal, i.e., correct, beliefs and practices. The liberal elites believe they know best what positions are correct on social issues, especially sexual mores. And in the latter case, the heavy hand of government intrusion is required.

Liberal parents, conversely, overwhelmingly view education as an opportunity to shape the minds of future citizens toward liberal, i.e., correct, beliefs and practices.

A classic case is the State of California's decision[14] to teach little children—as young as the second grade—about the contributions of LGBT individuals in history. Two social positions are thereby inculcated at an early age: first, status in a traditionally marginalized group carries more weight than the impact of the historical contributions themselves (also communicated by universities that eliminate core Western Civ classes to make room for classes—and degrees[15]—in gender studies); and second, liberal social positions are the only correct positions to have.

---

14 "California brings gay history into the classroom," *NPR*, July 22, 2011, http://www.npr.org/2011/07/22/138504488/california-brings-gay-history-into-the-classroom.

15 The website for U.C. Berkeley, Gender and Women's Studies, http://womensstudies.berkeley.edu/.

The LGBT influence on our society is complex and difficult enough for adults to navigate. If education is meant to prepare children for their future, one would expect schools to teach the full range of attitudes about sexual orientation and its manifestation. Or, better yet, none at all. The result of normalizing LGBT everything for 7-year-olds—and I believe strongly the intent—is to invalidate any other point of view or timing of the teaching according to each child's needs and maturity level.

If parents want to teach their children that homosexuality is beautiful and natural, but prefer to wait until their children are a little bit older, too bad. If parents want to teach their children that all people are beloved children of God, but He has given us commandments for how He wants us to relate to Him and to each other, too bad. If parents want to teach their children that homosexuality is wrong, period, that there are no exceptions, too bad.

When the government has the *prerogative*[16] to decide which social positions are correct; the *authority* to teach all children the "correct" social positions (which, make no mistake, are conveyed as the only correct positions a decent person can hold); and the *power* to legally coerce parents to comply (as in no opt-out policies), the government is raising our children. If we happen to agree with the government's politically correct positions, great; if not, too bad.

When the government has the *prerogative* to decide which social positions are correct; the *authority* to teach all children the "correct" social positions (which, make no mistake, are conveyed as the only correct positions a decent person can hold); and the *power* to legally coerce parents to comply (as in no opt-out policies), the government is raising our children.

---

16 "Your children belong to the State: Federal government tells parents they are inferior," *Instapundit*, January 1, 2015, http://pjmedia.com/instapundit/223158/.

As scary as the government's intrusion into our children's minds is, their intrusion into our children's most intimate behavior and future health (physical and emotional) is absolutely heinous. The ultimate government intrusion is permitting a fourteen-year-old girl to obtain an abortion without her parents' knowledge or permission.

Imagine. The parents of a 14-year-old girl have no idea that she is sexually active. When she becomes pregnant—arguably the most difficult situation of her young life and one which her parents are more qualified to guide her through than anyone else—she tells her teacher instead. The teacher, a well-meaning individual, takes it on faith when the girl says her parents will beat her or kick her out if they find out. (Perhaps the girl will only lose her cell phone, driving privileges, and unsupervised friend time, but to her, it's the end of the world, and she communicates it as such to her teacher.)

Of course, there are some parents who will beat their daughter and kick her out, but can we all agree that they are few and far between? Disappointed, heartbroken, and furious parents manage every day all over the world to control their reactions and act in their children's best interest. Yet the liberal elite get to decide for you what is in your child's best interest. From Planned Parenthood[17]:

> *You can ask a judge to excuse you from getting permission or telling your parent or guardian. In some states, you can be excused from involving a parent without going to a judge if you are the victim of abuse or neglect and you or your doctor report this to the appropriate authorities. If you are facing a medical emergency and require an immediate abortion, most states will not impose their parental involvement requirements.*

---

17 "Parental consent and notification laws," Planned Parenthood, accessed December 15, 2015, https://www.plannedparenthood.org/learn/abortion/parental-consent-notification-laws.

Abortion is a medical procedure with physical and emotional risks, including depression, infertility, and death. We would never countenance a doctor removing a child's limb without the parents' permission. A school nurse cannot administer an aspirin to a child without parental permission. But the government sees no problem with a doctor removing a human being in-the-making inside our child without our permission.

A school nurse cannot administer an aspirin to a child without parental permission. But the government sees no problem with a doctor removing a human being in-the-making inside our child without our permission.

We need a president who sees governmental usurpation of parental control as the lunacy it is. We need a president who protects the power of parents—all parents—to raise their children as they see fit. We need a president who keeps government out of our homes.

We need a president who keeps government out of our homes.

THE WAR
ON WOMEN

How does the candidate define the war on women?

If you Google "war on women[18]," the search engine gods return the following definition: *War on Women is an expression in United States politics used to describe certain Republican Party policies and legislation as a wide-scale effort to restrict women's rights, especially reproductive rights.*

War on Women is an expression in United States politics used to describe certain Republican Party policies and legislation as a wide-scale effort to restrict women's rights, especially reproductive rights.

If state legislatures enacting abortion restrictions is war, what do we call a thousand men sexually assaulting[19] more than a hundred women on New

---

18   *Wikipedia*, s.v. "War on Women," accessed February 1, 2016, https://en.wikipedia.org/wiki/War_on_Women.

19   "Cologne sex attacks: Women describe 'terrible' assaults," *BBC News*, January 7, 2016, http://www.bbc.com/news/world-europe-35250903.

Year's Eve in Cologne, Germany? If "certain Republican Party policies and legislation" are "a wide-scale effort to restrict women's rights, especially reproductive rights," why would any Republican women support these policies and legislation? If Obamacare covers every woman (who needs it) with subsidized contraception, where is the war? If employers could get the same exact work from women for 23 cents less on the dollar, why wouldn't soulless Big Business hire nothing but women and rock their bottom line?

Methinks I smell a rat.

Abortion

Full disclosure: I have had an abortion. When I was 28 and married and my husband said, "I don't want a baby, but it's your decision," and my Berkeley girlfriends said, "Go ahead, every woman gets one abortion. You can have your kids later." With no other perspective to consider, I couldn't wait to get what felt like an alien thing inside of me out of me. It was to me only a clump of cells.

Nearly 30 years later, I would give anything to take back that decision. I had never encountered the view that such a "clump of cells" was a child of God in-the-making. I can't think too long on how I ache to have known then what I know now, or I will lose my mind. More full disclosure: I can't swear it would have changed my decision if I had known. I would like to think it would, but I remember how desperate I was to get rid of it, so I will never know.

I have empathy for both the pro-choice and pro-life positions. I am passionately pro-life but feel strongly that abortions should be safe, legal, and rare. The subject is highly personal, profoundly intimate, and, to some of us, deeply spiritual, but it's not a war. How can it be a war when so many of us will find ourselves on different sides of the issue at different times in our lives? Am I at war with my 28-year-old self because my 50-something self doesn't agree with her decision? Of course not. I see it through different eyes now, but I have compassion for the younger me and why she made the choice she did. According to a Gallup poll in May, 2015[20], women middle-aged and older are more likely to be pro-choice today than they were in 2001; are they at war with their younger pro-life selves? Of course not.

I have empathy for both the pro-choice and pro-life positions. I am passionately pro-life but feel strongly that abortions should be safe, legal, and rare. The subject is highly personal, profoundly intimate, and, to some of us, deeply spiritual, but it's not a war.

There is no war; there is disagreement. If disagreement breaks along political lines, so, too, does marriage, an institution that exerts tremendous influence on the choices women make about contraception, pregnancy, and abortion. Republican women are far more likely to be married[21] than their Democrat sisters. There is no war; there is increase in the number of abortion restrictions to match the increase in our scientific knowledge. The earlier in a pregnancy the fetus is viable, the earlier in a pregnancy we must decide the moral full stop on termination.

---

20   Lydia Saad, "Americans choose 'pro-choice' for first time in seven years," *Gallup*, May 29, 2015, http://www.gallup.com/poll/183434/americans-choose-pro-choice-first-time-seven-years.aspx.

21   Jonathan Vankin, "Republicans and women: Single women vote democratic because they wish they were married, pundit says," *Inquisitr*, August 31, 2014, http://www.inquisitr.com/1443847/unmarried-women-republican/.

There is no war. No one throws acid in our faces if we seek an education. No one beheads us if we step outside our religion and date a person of another faith. We're allowed to vote[22] in national elections and hold national public office.

There is no war.

There is no war. What there is, is the Greatest Show on Earth—a bit Cirque Du Soleil, a bit David Copperfield— that sets up its tent during every presidential election.

What there is, is the Greatest Show on Earth—a bit Cirque Du Soleil, a bit David Copperfield—that sets up its tent during every presidential election. Pro-life as well as pro-choice candidates are guilty of whipping the crowds into a frenzy, trying to ride that wave into office. They play on women's emotional nature, inciting in us fear, outrage, and self- righteousness. What the ringmasters hope we won't notice is that it's all an illusion; nothing ever really changes.

Public opinion toward abortion has a life of its own; always has, always will. From the mid-1990s to 2009, a majority of Americans were pro-choice overall; from 2010 to 2014, a majority of Americans were pro-life; as of 2015, the pro-choice position is again more popular[23],

---

22 "Saudi Arabia's suffragettes: An electoral breakthrough for women in the Kingdom," *Wall Street Journal*, December 13, 2015, http://www.wsj.com/articles/saudi-arabias-suffragettes-1450047918.

23 Lydia Saad, "Americans choose 'pro-choice' for first time in seven years," *Gallup*, May 29, 2015, http://www.gallup.com/poll/183434/americans-choose-pro-choice-first-time-seven-years.aspx.

but polling shows a majority of millennials (59 percent) are pro-life[24]. With new controversies about personhood, late-term abortions, stem cell research, and the sale of aborted dead baby parts, this is going to go on and on. Still, these are only tiny up and down swells in a vast expanse of ocean called Roe v. Wade.

Nothing and no one is going to overturn Roe v. Wade. Even with archly conservative presidents in office since the 1973 Roe decision, the right of women to a safe, legal abortion has never been at risk. It's not a real issue. So why does anyone want us to think it is?

Nothing and no one is going to overturn Roe v. Wade. Even with archly conservative presidents in office since the 1973 Roe decision, the right of women to a safe, legal abortion has never been at risk. It's not a real issue. So why does anyone want us to think it is?

Politicians manipulate us through our emotions, and once they get us riled up, they also try to convince us they're the solution to our problems.

Politicians manipulate us through our emotions, and once they get us riled up, they also try to convince us they're the solution to our problems. When you're frightened, someone in power who says they can help you is a pretty powerful draw. Gender scholars have done a bang-up job of convincing

---

24   Cheryl Wetzstein, "Millennials bucking trends on abortion approval," *Washington Times*, January 25, 2015, http://www.washingtontimes.com/news/2015/jan/25/millennials-bucking-trends-on-abortion-approval/.

women that we're living in a state of siege, and that we need protection from men. Politicians—who never let a crisis go to waste—take full advantage of our fear to promise they will save us…but only if we vote for them.

Abortion is not a real issue. Don't follow the shiny object. Keep your eye on the ball.

Birth Control

First of all, most of us can pay for our own contraceptives without the help of insurance. Condoms are the cheapest, roughly $5 a month, and are often handed out free at certain clinics. The price rises through diaphragm, cervical cap, and IUD, to the most expensive option—about $50 a month for the Pill. Please don't tell me American women in 21st century America can't figure out how to get a free condom. Most of us can afford more than that.

For those of us who can't pay for our own contraceptives, there's Obamacare. For employees whose employers do not wish to cover contraceptives under their group health insurance, Obamacare makes it possible to buy them directly from the insurer for the same cost.

Birth control is cheap! And no one is left out.

Where's the war?

The Gender Pay Gap

The Gender Pay Gap has been debunked so many times that if you aren't aware of it, you need to get out more. I could spend an entire book on it, but here are the highlights:

- The 77 cents on the dollar gap between men and women is calculated by dividing the pay of *all* men by the pay of *all* women in *all* jobs nationwide.

- Many women choose to balance work and family by working part-time, or in less demanding jobs that require less education and training; they may also take extended breaks from the labor force to care for very young children. And many choose to work at jobs with flexible hours so they can be available when their families need them. When those factors are figured into the calculation, the gap shrinks to effectively zero.

- Women engineers are said to make less than their male counterparts, but this is an artifact of choice as well. Men tend to pick the highest-paying fields of engineering—petroleum and aeronautical—while women overwhelmingly choose the lowest-paying fields—environmental and biomedical.

- Women doctors reportedly make less than their male counterparts, but again, the operative variable is choice. Women tend to prefer[25] lower-paid medical specialties that require less time in school and can be practiced Monday-Friday, 9-5, e.g., Family Medicine, Psychiatry, Pediatrics, Dermatology. Men, on the other hand, are much more likely to choose high pressure, higher-paid specialties that require extra years of education or training, e.g., Neurosurgery, Emergency Medicine, Anesthesiology, and Radiology.

The war on women is a sand trap because it distracts us from real issues like ISIS and illegal immigration. Don't let anyone pull you into that sand trap. We need a president who speaks to our intellect on real issues rather than seeks to incite our emotions on ginned up hoo-ha.

---

25 "How medical specialties vary by gender," *AMA Wire*, February 18, 2015, http://www.ama-assn.org/ama/ama-wire/post/medical-specialties-vary-gender.

The war on women is a sand trap because it distracts us from real issues like ISIS and illegal immigration. Don't let anyone pull you into that sand trap. As Camille Paglia says, "Read widely and think for yourself." Women are the majority of citizens and the majority of voters. We need a president who speaks to our intellect on real issues rather than seeks to incite our emotions on ginned up hoo-ha.

TERRORISM
—THE ISIS KIND

How does the candidate plan to manage and respond to ISIS at home and abroad?

The correct response to terrorism is simple. Not easy, simple.
Identify the problem correctly;
Solve the problem correctly; and
Prevent future instances of the problem correctly.

"You Can't Fix What You Don't Acknowledge."—Dr. Phil

If it walks like a duck and quacks like a duck, it's a duck. If it uses violence and intimidation to pursue its political aims, it's terrorism. President Obama can call it workplace violence all he wants, but if it scares us into changing our daily lives, it's terrorism.

Workplace violence … they used to call it "going postal[26]." Back in the '80s and '90s, seriously stressed postal workers shot and killed co-workers,

---

26   *Wikipedia*, s.v. "Going Postal," accessed February 6, 2016, https://en.wikipedia.org/wiki/Going_postal.

bosses, customers, and police officers. (As an aside, now that we've all seen *American* Sniper, working with letters and packages and civil servant bosses doesn't seem so stressful, does it?)

Workplace violence is a new catchall term that means: 1) some people were killed at work; 2) the motive of the shooter(s) is irrelevant; 3) the religious influences on the shooter(s) are irrelevant; and 3) we don't need to do anything but clean up the blood. And call for more gun control, natch.

"Workplace violence" is a political olly olly oxen free where would-be terrorists—deftly reframed as disgruntled or unstable employees—are free to commit mayhem. The shooters are overwhelmingly young, male, and of Middle Eastern culture or descent. They also—wait for it—have some connection[27] to radical Islam. Today's workplace violence is not your father's workplace violence. In the old days, all anyone needed was a gun and a shot at a supervisor's head (and maybe the supervisor's boyfriend's head). Today's workplace violence can mean body armor, automatic weapons, GoPros, and hundreds of rounds of ammunition.

Back in the day, the cause (problems with someone at work) and the effect (injury or death to that someone) were directly and logically connected. Today we're asked to believe that interpersonal problems at work are truly the cause of beheadings[28] and mass murder[29].

---

27 Marcy Kreiter, "Fort Hood shooter Nidal Malik Hasan wants to join ISIS, become a citizen," *International Business Times*, August 30, 2014, http://www.ibtimes.com/fort-hood-shooter-nidal-malik-hasan-wants-join-isis-become-citizen-1674538.

28 "Police: Woman beheaded at Oklahoma workplace," *CBS News*, last modified September 26, 2014, accessed January 31, 2016, http://www.cbsnews.com/news/police-woman-beheaded-at-oklahoma-workplace/.

29 Michael Foust, "14 killed in terrorism-style shooting in San Bernardino; Christian leaders urge prayer," *Christian Examiner*, December 2, 2015, http://www.christianexaminer.com/article/14-killed-in-terrorism-style-shooting-in-san-bernardino-christian-leaders-urge-prayer/49872.htm.

Back in the day, the cause (problems with someone at work) and the effect (injury or death to that someone) were directly and logically connected. Today we're asked to believe that interpersonal problems at work are truly the cause of beheadings and mass murder.

Twitter (I just love Twitter), that repository of all things bitingly humorous, captured it thus:

Honey, I had an argument at the office. Can you put together a few dozen pipe bombs, get Go-Pros, body armor and assault rifles & meet in 15?

The issue is not that workplace violence sometimes looks like terrorism; it does. The issue is that no matter what violence and intimidation occur at work, they are never acknowledged as terrorism. An hour before the FBI declared[30] the Christmas party massacre in San Bernardino to be terrorism, the White House was still refusing to do so. One could be forgiven for erring on the side of caution—the hinterlands of caution—and withholding a declaration of Islamic terrorism until we have definitive proof. What undermines the credibility of those who would withhold such judgments—hail to the Chief, anyone?—is that even when the shooters(s) shout "Allahu Akbar" (God is the greatest) as they mow us down, officials do mental gymnastics declaring it anything but Islamic jihad.

---

30 "Now even Obama has to admit San Bernardino was terrorism," *New York Post,* December 4, 2015, http://nypost.com/2015/12/04/now-even-obama-has-to-admit-it-san-bernardino-was-terrorism/.

> One could be forgiven for erring on the side of caution—
> the hinterlands of caution—and withholding a declara-
> tion of Islamic terrorism until we have definitive proof.
> What undermines the credibility of those who would
> withhold such judgments—hail to the Chief, anyone?—is
> that even when the shooters(s) shout "Allahu Akbar" (God
> is the greatest) as they mow us down, officials do mental
> gymnastics declaring it anything but Islamic jihad.

When Major Nidal Hassan shot dozens of soldiers at Ft. Hood in 2009, he explicitly stated[31] that he was protecting Taliban soldiers in Afghanistan from American troops. And yet the official charges were murder, not terrorism. The Army's lead prosecutor couldn't even bring himself to use the word terrorism, referring to it as the "T-word" instead.

> The T-word? Really? The N-word, the A-word, the B-word,
> and the F-word aren't enough? Terrorism is the new he-who-
> must-not-be-named? How do we solve a problem we refuse
> to identify correctly?

A Hammer Won't Fix a Hole
Remember the old saw (pun intended) about having only a hammer in your workbench? You'll try to solve all problems with a hammer. Gun

---

31 Manny Fernandez and Alan Blinder, "At Ford Hood, wrestling with terrorism," *New York Times*, April 8, 2015, http://www.nytimes.com/2014/04/09/us/at-fort-hood-wrestling-with-label-of-terrorism.html.

control is our government's 21st century hammer. A mentally unstable young man shoots up a Colorado movie theater? More gun control. A mentally unstable young man shoots up an elementary school? More gun control. A young girl accidentally shoots her sister? More gun control. An out-of-control murder rate in Chicago? More gun control. A husband and wife abandon their 6-month-old daughter, don body armor, and use automatic weapons to mow down a Christmas party? I think you can guess.

Let's go with the gun control solution for a minute, just for grins. The basis of all gun control legislation is to restrict firearm access and to minimize loss of life or limb. We have laws[32] that prevent the mentally unstable from obtaining a gun. We have laws that prohibit civilians from obtaining assault weapons. We have laws that prevent minors from purchasing or owning a gun. We have waiting periods, background checks, and school zone bans.

Yet. Where there's a will, there's a way. The mentally unstable can break into their mother's gun cabinet. Assault weapons are clearly available to the truly determined. The only way to prevent minors from having gun accidents is to prevent them from accessing guns, anywhere, anytime, under any circumstances. Such utopia is theoretically possible only if all guns are banned, anywhere, anytime, under any circumstances, and it should be obvious by now that people who want guns aren't going to let gun laws stop them. Let's be real.

Additional gun restrictions not only don't solve the problem correctly, they make it worse. If you're hiding under your desk while bullets rain down, a Saturday night special is more likely to preserve life and limb than a (potentially impossible) call to 911. And how many people die before police arrive? How many are maimed? A bird in the hand is worth two in the bush.

---

32 "What are gun control laws?" Legal Match, accessed December 15, 2015, http://www.legalmatch.com/law-library/article/gun-control-laws.html.

If guns are the problem, why is it that when the good guys have them, the stories have happier endings? Because the CEO of Vaughan Foods had his gun with him on September 26, 2014—and used it[33]—he prevented Alton Nolen from beheading a second female employee. Because a good guy had a gun, Traci Johnson[34] was able to celebrate Christmas with her family instead of being buried in what would surely have been a closed casket. Just saying.

We need a president who recognizes terrorism for what it is, who is willing to call it what it is, and who puts the welfare of the American people above the politically correct how-will-it-play-in-the-polls-mentality that has become the norm. And wouldn't it be nice if we had president who used resources to keep us safe rather than to warn us against racial profiling?

And one look at Chicago will tell you that banning guns does not work. With some of the toughest gun laws in the country, Chicago still has the highest rate of gun violence. Then there's Paris. With some of the toughest gun laws in the entire world, terrorists in Paris were still able to access and use guns.

---

33 Jason Howerton, "It wasn't the police who neutralized alleged Muslim convert with bullets after beheading of woman in Oklahoma," *The Blaze*, September 26, 2014, http://www.theblaze.com/stories/2014/09/26/it-wasnt-the-police-who-neutralized-alleged-muslim-convert-with-bullets-after-he-beheaded-woman-in-oklahoma/.

34 "'He started slicing my neck:' Woman tells how she was almost beheaded by crazed grocery store co-worker who killed her colleague after he tried to convert them to Islam," *Daily Mail*, June 23, 2015, http://www.dailymail.co.uk/news/article-3136624/He-started-slicing-neck-got-millimeter-jugular-Woman-beheaded-crazed-worker-killed-speaks-nine-months-on.html.

One look at Chicago will tell you that banning guns does not work. With some of the toughest gun laws in the country, Chicago still has the highest rate of gun violence.

Don't Learn From the Past? Condemned to Repeat It

If the problem isn't workplace violence, and the solution isn't more gun control, how do we prevent future occurrences? The answer is, we don't. Let's imagine, just for grins, that we do identify the problem correctly—terrorism committed by radicalized fundamentalist Islamic jihadis; we solve the problem correctly—empower individual citizens to protect themselves and their families with legally obtained firearms. Now, how do we prevent future occurrences?

The answer is simple. Again, not easy, simple. The chain of events that results in an act of terrorism follows a logical sequence; the clues are not even as difficult as the New York

Times Sunday Crossword Puzzle. The parts of the terrorism puzzle are Who, What, When, Where, and Why.

- **Who** – radicalized fundamentalist Islamic jihadis
- **What** – assault weapons, IEDs, body armor (GoPros optional)
- **When** – ordinary people are gathered together for innocent purposes
- **Where** – no place off-limits
- **Why** – kill and maim us to please Allah

We can prevent future occurrences of terrorism by controlling for the above variables. Let's toss out the ones that are impossible to control—when, where, and why. That leaves what and who.

How can we control the variable of what? If determined terrorists can eventually obtain assault weapons, IEDs, and body armor, then laws to restrict these elements will accomplish only so much. Kind of like holding Kleenex over a hemorrhage to slow the bleeding. I give Homeland Security the benefit of the doubt that they infiltrate and monitor terror cells to stem the flow of weapons and ammunition. I'm sure that so far above my pay grade I can't even fathom who they are, other people are engaged in other ways to combat terrorism. As ordinary citizens, we have limited usefulness in the *what* arena; where we can make a difference is in the *who*.

How can we control the variable of who? Obviously we exercise control over who commits terror by identifying potential terror suspects and blocking their opportunities. This begs the question of how radicalized fundamentalist Islamic jihadis come to be. Obviously baby radicalized fundamentalist Islamic jihadis are born and nurtured by more experienced radicalized fundamentalist Islamic jihadis. Where do radicalized fundamentalist Islamic jihadis congregate? In countries overrun by ISIS; in cultures that align with the values of killing and maiming to please Allah; in western mosques that are radicalized or offer cover for below-the-radar jihadis; and on the Internet.

Controlling the variable of who is one of the most explosive problems we face today. Like abortion, the death penalty, and illegal immigration, our views vary dramatically. One end of the spectrum is the view that radical Islamic terrorism is a ruse cooked up by our own government to destabilize the country and seize more power for itself. The other end of the spectrum is the view that all Muslims are terrorists. Most of us eschew either extreme.

I don't have the complete answer to how we control who, and I don't believe the people above my pay grade do either. Each new attack gives us more information on who, what, when, where, and why; each new attack also polarizes the divide between those who call it workplace violence and those who call it terrorism.

The truth is, we're still figuring it out. Do we take in Syrian refugees who are mostly innocent victims? Or do we keep them out to also keep out the terrorists-posing-as-refugees with an evil job to do? There are reasonable arguments to be made on either side.

We need a president who is willing to identify the problem correctly; who is committed to solving the problem correctly; who is prepared to admit that we may presently be going about it in the wrong way; and who is strong enough to double down on our present methods if that's the way we decide to go. We need a president who recognizes terrorism for what it is, who is willing to call it what it is, and who puts the welfare of the American people above the politically correct how-will-it-play-in-the-polls-mentality that has become the norm. And wouldn't it be nice if we had president who used resources to keep us safe rather than to warn us against racial profiling?

FOREIGN POLICY: DO WE BOMB INNOCENT CIVILIANS OR NOT?

Will the candidate do whatever it takes to keep America safe, or will s/he stop short of killing innocent women and children?

This is the most contentious of all the questions, even more so than abortion. In abortion, one side disputes that the "clump of cells" is even a human life; in questions of foreign policy, both sides are well aware that every victim is a human being full of hopes and dreams.

In modern memory, this dilemma arose when we dropped the atom bomb on Hiroshima in 1945. To force Japan's surrender, we allowed 70,000 of their citizens to be instantly vaporized[35] and another 100,000 to die slow and painful deaths from burns and radiation sickness. Three days later, we

---

35 "The decision to drop the bomb," *U.S. History*, accessed January 1, 2016, http://www.ushistory.org/us/51g.asp.

dropped a similar bomb on Nagasaki with the same instant vaporization, burns, and radiation sickness on a slightly smaller scale. President Truman, whose call it was to use the bombs, admitted it was the most difficult decision of his life.

From that moment on, Americans have been deeply divided over the use of nuclear weapons, especially against civilians. Immediately after the attacks, 85 percent of Americans polled by the Pew Research Group felt the attacks were justified[36] in order to end the war and save American lives. Seventy years later in 2005, only 56 percent felt we were justified in killing Japanese civilians to save ourselves.

Today, we face the same dilemma in the Middle East. At a speech on December 5, 2015, Republican presidential candidate Ted Cruz advocated "carpet bombing" ISIS[37] "into oblivion." He wondered if sand could glow in the dark, and promised we would find out if he were elected president. Cruz's poll numbers rose after the comments, prompting the Nation to publish an article subtitled "How do we explain Americans' lack of empathy for those on the other end of our bombing campaigns?" That is certainly one way to frame it.

Cruz immediately clarified that he would not bomb the ISIS capital city of Raqqah where there would be many civilian casualties. "You would carpet bomb where ISIS is, not a city, but the location of the troops."

Doesn't it sound a bit wishful to imagine targeted bombing of ISIS terrorists only? Since ISIS embeds itself in cities, going after ISIS terrorists

---

36 "The REAL reason America used nuclear weapons against Japan (it was not to end the war or save lives), *WashingtonsBlogs*, October 14, 2012, http://www.washingtonsblog. com/2012/10/the-real-reason-america-used-nuclear-weapons-against-japan-to-contain-russian-ambitions.html.

37 Louis Jacobson, "Ted Cruz misfires on definition of 'carpet bombing' in GOP debate," *Politifact*, December 16, 2015, http://www.politifact.com/truth-o-meter/statements/2015/dec/16/ted-cruz/ted-cruz-misfires-definition-carpet-bombing-gop-de/.

inevitably means civilian casualties as well. Are we willing to do that? Are we willing to proclaim that the safety and well-being of the American people is worth the deaths of large numbers of innocent civilians? Or will we pull our punches to protect civilians made vulnerable because ISIS is using them as human shields? Are we allowed to proclaim our culture superior to others in the Middle East and therefore worth saving at all costs? I don't know.

I'm willing to consider any strategy, but I agree in principle that we are allowed to defend ourselves, attack those trying to kill us, and preserve our way of life by any means necessary. The only reason we wouldn't—and this is deep—is to atone for our sins. If we are the evil country that President Obama described in his 2008 worldwide apology tour[38], we aren't worthy of continued existence.

Doesn't it sound a bit wishful to imagine targeted bombing of ISIS terrorists only? Since ISIS embeds itself in cities, going after ISIS terrorists inevitably means civilian casualties as well. Are we willing to do that? Are we willing to proclaim that the safety and well-being of the American people is worth the deaths of large numbers of innocent civilians?

Indeed #AmericanLivesDON'TMatter because we are sexist, intolerant, xenophobic, homophobic, racist, bigoted, imperialist, classist, and privileged. From this point of view, we are expected to fall on our sword and let someone

---

38 Karl Rove, "The President's apology tour," *Wall Street Journal*, April 23, 2009, http://www.wsj.com/articles/SB124044156269345357.

else have a turn because we've already hogged more than our share of stuff for way too long. Not only do we not carpet bomb anyone, we elevate the enemy's culture/religion/social customs above our own. We don't last long as a society, but we don't deserve to, so it's okay.

If, on the other hand, American Exceptionalism is true—along with our many flaws, weaknesses, and mistakes—we have the right to survive, even if it means killing innocents our enemy hides behind to prevent us from killing him, or at least make us look evil for killing him. I would argue that we have a *duty* to survive because of what we have to offer the rest of the world. I noticed that President Obama did not apologize to descendants of Holocaust survivors for our liberation of concentration camps at the end of WWII. He also didn't apologize for the billions of dollars[39] we give in aid all over the world every year.

How we answer the fundamental question—do we deserve to survive—dictates our foreign policy toward regimes intent on our humiliation and destruction. If we don't deserve to survive, the president will omit in his State of the Union Address any mention of the ten sailors Iran seized[40] only hours before. We will thank Iran for releasing the sailors even though they're keeping five other American hostages. We will say nothing when they mock us with a photo of our brave young sailors kneeling with their hands behind their heads like common criminals. When they release a

---

39 Becket Adams, "$37,680,000,000: That's how much the U.S. spent on foreign aid in 2012: Here's a chart that helps explain it," *The Blaze*, December 19, 2013, http://www.theblaze.com/stories/2013/12/19/37680000000-thats-how-much-the-u-s-spends-on-foreign-aid-heres-a-chart-that-helps-explain-it/.

40 Jim Miklaszewski and Courtney Kube, "Pentagon: 2 U.S. Navy boats with 10 American sailors held by Iran military," *NBC News*, January 12, 2016, http://www.nbcnews.com/news/world/pentagon-2-u-s-navy-boats-held-iran-military-n495031.

video[41] of their American captives apologizing for the "mistake" they made entering Iranian-controlled waters, we will simply ignore it and continue to emphasize our cordial relations.

If we do deserve to survive as a culture, and I maintain unequivocally that we do, cordial relations will be a two-way street, not a PR activity. Provocations and humiliations by unfriendly regimes will receive swift response. Swift, strong, and self-respecting.

If we do deserve to survive as a culture, and I maintain unequivocally that we do, cordial relations will be a two-way street, not a PR activity. Provocations and humiliations by unfriendly regimes will receive swift response. Swift, strong, and self-respecting.

When my daughter was fourteen, a boy in her junior high walked behind her in the halls, kicking her legs and giving her what we used to call "flat tires." He was constantly there after every class; pleading with him, reporting him to the principal, and avoiding him didn't work. In fact, it emboldened him.

The school handbook read—I kid you not—"We live in a world where it's not safe to defend ourselves." (That has got to be the single most asinine thing I have ever heard.) I stepped out of my Girl Scout, rule-following, obedience-to-authority self long enough to tell my daughter:

---

41 Todd Beamon, Iran releases video of US sailor's apology for mishap in Persian Gulf," *Newsmax*, January 13, 2016, http://www.newsmax.com/Newsfront/sailors-iran-boat-state-of-the-union/2016/01/13/id/709337/.

"If this kid does it again, turn around very calmly and say, 'My mom says if you do that again, I have her permission to punch you in the stomach as hard as I can, and if I do, she will take me out to lunch.'"

He did it again, she punched him, I took her out to lunch, and he never bothered her again. She also carried herself with a lot more confidence after that, and purely coincidentally I'm sure, has not been bullied since by anyone else either. I was almost hoping she would get in trouble with the school for doing it so that I could give them a piece of my mind about how *not* to handle bullies. Fortunately or unfortunately for all of us, the opportunity did not present itself.

America is an asset in the world and to the world. We deserve to survive and even thrive because we are exceptional. More importantly, when we thrive, we bring others with us. We used to hold our heads high. We used to have our allies' backs. We used to be respected. It's not too late to have that again.

We need a president who knows we're the good guys and isn't afraid to back that up with a little firepower when necessary.

America is an asset in the world and to the world. We deserve to survive and even thrive because we are exceptional. More importantly, when we thrive, we bring others with us. We used to hold our heads high. We used to have our allies' backs. We used to be respected. It's not too late to have that again.

ILLEGAL IMMIGRATION

What is the candidate's plan to solve our immigration crisis?

D ebate in our country over illegal immigration burns white-hot—even the words "illegal immigrant" are bitterly contested. Large majorities of Americans favor allowing illegal immigrants to remain here with a path to citizenship, but enough of the frustrated minority may propel Donald Trump into the presidency. It is such a complicated issue, so fraught with emotion, that many of us don't even know what to think. I am one of those.

Where do we draw the line between enforcing our laws—deporting people who have entered our country illegally—and breaking families apart by separating parents from children? Some would say we deport the kids with the parents, but many of those kids were born on American soil and are American citizens. We can't deport American citizens, can we?

From my armchair quarterback position, I see three critical pieces to step one of immigration reform: seal the borders, enforce existing laws, and reject the "anchor baby" interpretation of the Fourteenth Amendment that allows children born here under any circumstances to gain American citizenship. It wouldn't hurt to require that any legal immigrants show self-sufficiency and the ability to make tangible contributions to our society. Step two is to decide what to do with those already here.

Seal the borders, enforce existing laws, and reject the "anchor baby" interpretation of the Fourteenth Amendment that allows children born here under any circumstances to gain American citizenship. It wouldn't hurt to require that any legal immigrants show self-sufficiency and the ability to make tangible contributions to our society.

There is no perfect solution; there is only the lesser of many evils, and I still don't know what that is. Each candidate will put forward a plan for immigration reform, and the best we can do is to evaluate each plan in light of the following:

Clarification of Terms

Back in the day, we called non-citizens who were present in our country unlawfully or without our authorization "illegal immigrants[42]"; that term has fallen out of usage, to be replaced with "illegal immigrant," "undocumented immigrant," "unauthorized migrant," or the increasingly popular "undocumented worker."

---

42   Ilona Bray, JD, "Who is an undocumented immigrant?" *Nolo Press*, accessed February 1, 2016, http://www.nolo.com/legal-encyclopedia/who-is-undocumented-immigrant.html.

- Illegal Immigrant – today's version of illegal alien.
- Undocumented immigrant[43] – foreign-born person who doesn't have a legal right to be or remain in the United States.
- Unauthorized Migrant[44] – someone who is moving across national borders, about whose legal status no presumption is made.
- Undocumented Worker[45] – who does not have proper documents for U.S. residency or for employment, whatever the reason.

The language we choose frames the debate and belies our personal beliefs. In "Words That Work: It's Not What You Say, It's What People Hear," political consultant Frank Luntz "advocates the term "illegal immigrant" over "undocumented worker." His job, he says, is to turn public opinion for his clients—in this case the Republican Party. Advocates for immigration reform and Hispanic media organizations maintain that "illegal immigrant" is dehumanizing and racialized. These parties, similarly, want to turn public opinion to their views.

The language we choose frames the debate and belies our personal beliefs.

---

43 Ibid.

44 Gene Dembey, "In immigration debate, 'undocumented' vs. 'illegal' is more than just semantics," *NPR*, January 30, 2013, http://www.npr.org/sections/itsall-politics/2013/01/30/170677880/in-immigration-debate-undocumented-vs-illegal-is-more-than-just-semantics.

45 Felix Salmon, "The 'illegal' index: Which news organization still use the term 'illegal immigrant?'" *Fusion*, November 20, 2014, http://fusion.net/story/28845/the-illegal-index/.

A 2012 poll by Fox News Latino[46] found that 46 percent of Latino voters think "illegal immigrants" is offensive while a little over a third said they thought it was accurate. As of April 2013, the Associated Press abandoned the term[47] in all of its published stories, indicating along with Hispanic media organizations that the term criminalizes people rather than their actions, and stigmatizes both immigrants and Hispanics. In a series of predictable dominos, the New York Times announced[48] within hours that it would review its use of the term; USA Today, the country's second-largest newspaper by circulation, followed in AP's footsteps[49] a week later.

The tide continues to turn against "illegal immigrant." An oft-repeated rationale among Immigrants' Rights groups is that we don't call people with traffic violations "illegal drivers[50]," so why would we call people with immigration violations "illegal immigrants?" A second rationale is that "illegal immigrant" does not cover the many foreign nationals who entered our country legally and then overstayed their Visas[51].

---

46   Andrew O'Reilly, "Undocumented or illegal: Media outlets battle over immigration terms," *Fox News Latino*, September 25, 2012, http://latino.foxnews.com/latino/news/2012/09/25/undocumented-or-illegal-media-outlets-battle-over-immigration-terms/.

47   Roque Planas, "AP drops term 'illegal immigrant' from style guide, *Huffington Post*, April 2, 2013, http://www.huffingtonpost.com/2013/04/02/ap-drops-term-illegal-immigrant_n_3001432.html.

48   Margaret Sullivan, "The Times, too, is reconsidering the term 'illegal immigrant," *New York Times*, April 2, 2013, http://publiceditor.blogs.nytimes.com/2013/04/02/the-times-too-is-reconsidering-the-term-illegal-immigrant/.

49   Roque Planas, "USA Today drops 'illegal immigrant,'" *Huffington Post*, April 11, 2013, http://www.huffingtonpost.com/2013/04/11/usa-today-illegal-immigrant_n_3062479.html.

50   Felix Salmon, "The 'illegal' index: Which news organization still use the term 'illegal immigrant?'" *Fusion*, November 20, 2014, http://fusion.net/story/28845/the-illegal-index/.

51   Gene Dembey, "In immigration debate, 'undocumented' vs. 'illegal' is more than just semantics," *NPR*, January 30, 2013, http://www.npr.org/sections/itsallpolitics/2013/01/30/170677880/in-immigration-debate-undocumented-vs-illegal-is-more-than-just-semantics.

I vote for logic.

I vote for logic. We don't call people who speed "illegal drivers," but we call people without auto insurance "criminals." We don't call people who haven't filed their taxes "illegal filers," but we call people who refuse to obey our tax laws "criminals." Wesley Snipes served jail time[52] for claiming his foreign earnings were exempt from taxation and declining to file a return from 1999 to 2001.

Entering our country illegally is a criminal offense; overstaying one's visa is a civil offense. One type of immigrant starts as a criminal and remains so; one type starts as a law-abiding resident and steps outside the law as soon as he declines to leave when his visa expires. If we as a society choose to assign consequences to "criminal immigrants" than "civil violation immigrants," so be it. But can we please take the marbles out of our mouths and just call them all illegal immigrants? After all, we can call "vehicular homicide" a "hit and run" and nobody gets their undies in a wad.

Entering our country illegally is a criminal offense; overstaying one's visa is a civil offense. One type of immigrant starts as a criminal and remains so; one type starts as a law-abiding resident and steps outside the law as soon as he declines to leave when his visa expires. But can we please take the marbles out of our mouths and just call them all illegal immigrants? After all, we can call "vehicular homicide" a "hit and run" and nobody gets their undies in a wad.

---

52 Ann Oldenburg, "Wesley Snipes finishes prison time for tax evasion," *USA Today*, 04/05/2013, http://www.usatoday.com/story/life/people/2013/04/05/wesley-snipes-finishes-jail-time-for-tax-evasion/2057455/.

History and Politics of Illegal Immigration

Illegal immigration in the U.S. was born in 1875 when we passed the first federal law[53] prohibiting the entry of convicts and prostitutes. The story of illegal immigration ever since has been one of messy politics and racism, powerful incentives, and the American Dream. The Irish, the Italians, the Japanese, Catholics, and Jews all endured their turn at rejection. Today the hottest and whitest debate over illegal immigration concerns Latin America.

The politics of Latin American Immigration[54] start as far back as the Roman Empire. (I promise this will not be boring.) By the time Columbus sailed to the New World, Spain had revived the Roman political system, while England was imbued with the values of their Saxon forebears who fought vigorously against arbitrary rule (the kind exercised by the Caesars in Rome). Both colonial powers bequeathed their respective political systems to their colonies.

Handed down to the U.S. and Canada by England was a system of liberty: individuals had rights; freemen could own property; leaders were often elected and served at the will of the people; kings were subject to the same laws as the common man; and the government exercised limited control over the economy, i.e., free-market economics reigned. In North America, freedom and prosperity for the society as a whole was a direct result of freedom and prosperity for the individual.

Handed down to Latin America by Spain was a system of authoritarian rule by the state in the form of kings (first) then despots (later): individuals

---

53 "Focus on your mission," *End Illegal Immigration*, April 11, 2012, http://www.endillegalimmigration.com/Illegal_Immigration_Laws/index.shtml.

54 John L. Hancock, "The border between the U.S. and Mexico is more than just a line on the map," *Breitbart*, June 12, 2015, http://www.breitbart.com/big-government/2015/06/12/the-border-between-the-u-s-and-mexico-is-more-than-just-a-line-on-the-map/.

had no rights, not even to life itself; kings had complete control over their subjects and were subject to nothing but their own whim; the common people were chattel whose purpose it was to serve the elites; and the highly centralized government controlled virtually all economic activity, i.e., the common man's duty was to obey the king and pay his taxes. In Latin America, the lack of freedom and prosperity for the society as a whole is a direct result of subjugation and economic stagnation for the individual. There's a reason Spain retained a peasant class until the 1970s; Latin America still has one.

Our system of liberty produced Washington, Jefferson, and Adams; Latin America's system of authoritarian rule produced Santa Ana, Castro, and Chavez. Our country is known for its political stability; Latin America is infamous for its political instability. North of the Mexican border, the American dream is still a possibility for everyday people. South of the Mexican border, dreams come true for only an elite, wealthy few.

Our system of liberty produced Washington, Jefferson, and Adams; Latin America's system of authoritarian rule produced Santa Ana, Castro, and Chavez. Our country is known for its political stability; Latin America is infamous for its political instability. North of the Mexican border, the American dream is still a possibility for everyday people. South of the Mexican border, dreams come true for only an elite, wealthy few.

Whether Latin American immigrants are legal, illegal, or "undocumented," they bring with them a cultural ethos inimical to our own.

People everywhere do what they know, and unless we as a society take steps to reinforce our North American culture, we may see it diluted to the level of "all societies are equal."

People everywhere do what they know, and unless we as a society take steps to reinforce our North American culture, we may see it diluted to the level of "all societies are equal."

Obviously, all societies are not equal. Latin Americans are sneaking over the border to Arizona; Texans are not clamoring to be let into Mexico. Are we willing to proclaim our political system the best there ever was? Are we willing to require immigrants to learn our language, vote in English, and compete on a level playing field for available jobs? Or do we allow political correctness to ghettoize immigrants politically and economically by not requiring them to speak the official language of our society? Do we expect immigrants to identify publicly as Americans and form an integral part of our world? Or do we allow them to marginalize themselves by publicly exerting their ethnic identity with a hyphen, e.g. Mexican-American?

Are we willing to proclaim our political system the best there ever was? Are we willing to require immigrants to learn our language, vote in English, and compete on a level playing field for available jobs? Or do we allow political correctness to ghettoize immigrants politically and economically by not

---

> requiring them to speak the official language of our society?
> Do we expect immigrants to identify publicly as Americans
> and form an integral part of our world? Or do we allow them
> to marginalize themselves by publicly exerting their ethnic
> identity with a hyphen, e.g. Mexican-American?

Illegal Immigration Today and Tomorrow

In October 2015, a Pew research poll[55] found that 74 percent of Americans said "undocumented immigrants" should be allowed to remain in the country, and almost 50 percent said they supported full citizenship. Twenty-four percent of Americans said "undocumented immigrants" should be deported. It sounds decided, but given the power of carefully selected words to sway attitudes, I wonder how the results would have been different had the pollsters used the words "illegal immigrants."

It's a mess. It's a mess today, and it looks to be a mess for a long time to come. The only way forward is through it, and preferably with the horse before the cart. We can spend time today pondering the solution to our immigration problems of tomorrow, but without solving our immigration crisis today, pondering is all it is. We have to address an awful lot of immediate no-win situations before we can move forward.

Are we going to deport people? Whom? If we choose not to deport people, under what circumstances should they be allowed to remain legally in our country? Do we support a path to citizenship for them?

---

55 Sara Kehaulani Goo, "What Americans want to do about illegal immigration," *Pew Research Center*, August 24, 2015, http://www.pewresearch.org/fact-tank/2015/08/24/what-americans-want-to-do-about-illegal-immigration/.

Under what circumstances? How does their potential path to citizenship relate to the path to citizenship legal immigrants are expected to follow?

As anyone who has ever implemented a decision knows, half the proof of the decision is in the implementation. You don't spend future cash flows, and you don't make immigration policy from immigration reform plans.

I'm willing to consider any reasonable plan to resolve our border problems that requires immigrants to become full-fledged Americans.

I'm willing to consider any reasonable plan to resolve our border problems that requires immigrants to become full-fledged Americans.

THE ECONOMY AND SMALL BUSINESS REGULATION

What will the candidate do to make it easier for women entrepreneurs to start and run businesses?

D o you even know what's happening in the world of small business regulation? Unless you have a business or tried to start one in the last few years, probably not. It's crazy town. You may have heard about the two little girls in Texas who couldn't sell lemonade without a permit[56] and a license from the County Board of Health, but it's even worse than that. Since entrepreneurship is the new Women's Movement[57], I've assembled a cavalcade of the craziness for your consideration.

First, a little background. The U.S. defines "small business"[58] on an indus-

---

56   Avianne Tan, "Texas kids told 'it's illegal" to sell lemonade without a permit," *ABC News*, June 10, 2015, http://abcnews.go.com/US/texas-kids-told-illegal-sell-lemonade-permit/story?id=31667943.

57   Natalie MacNeal, "Entrepreneurship is the new Women's Movement, *Forbes*, June 8, 2012, http://www.forbes.com/sites/work-in-progress/2012/06/08/entrepreneurship-is-the-new-womens-movement/#730071026922

58   *Wikipedia*, s.v. "Small business," last modified February 2, 2016, accessed February 2, 2016, https://en.wikipedia.org/wiki/Small_business.

try-by-industry basis, but in general, small businesses are those that have up to 500 employees for manufacturing businesses and less than $7.5 million in annual receipts for non-manufacturing businesses.

Within the small business universe, women-owned businesses are where it's at[59]. In 2010, women-owned businesses created only 16 percent of all jobs nationwide; by 2018, women are expected to create more than half the 9.72 million new small business jobs. Minority-owned female businesses have increased by 265 percent since 1997.

Within the small business universe, women-owned businesses are where it's at. In 2010, women-owned businesses created only 16 percent of all jobs nationwide; by 2018, women are expected to create more than half the 9.72 million new small business jobs. Minority-owned female businesses have increased by 265 percent since 1997.

It's a little misleading to quote such a dramatic rise in minority-owned female businesses, because the number in 1997 was small. What's revealing about the increase is that the women who start new minority-owned businesses are the youngest group of women entrepreneurs; they're more tech savvy and better able to use online purchasing and social media to stay in touch with their customers. As of 2015, black women owned 14 percent and Hispanic women owned 11 percent of all female-headed small businesses.

---

59   Gillian B. White, "Women are owning more and more small businesses," *The Atlantic*, April 17, 2015, http://www.theatlantic.com/business/archive/2015/04/women-are-owning-more-and-more-small-businesses/390642/.

Women want work that aligns with our personal values and that allows more freedom and flexibility; we want our children to get the best of us, not the rest of us.

Women are more likely than men to start a small or home-based business. We want work that aligns with our personal values and that allows more freedom and flexibility; we want our children to get the best of us, not the rest of us. And, given the economy, many of us will have no other options.

Here are two things that don't go together: 1) women attempting to choose the life they want and provide for their families, an 2) the crushing weight and expense of gobs of small business regulations. In 2014, the Obama Administration signed 129 new small business laws[60] into action. Accompanying those 129 new laws were 3,541 new regulations; that's approximately 27 new regulations per law[61]. And this number doesn't take into account all the new de facto laws implemented by government bulletins, guidance documents, blog posts, press conferences, and the ever-ready phone and pen.

A few[62] of the more laughable-if-they-weren't-so painful regulations:

---

60 "NFIB declares support for two new House bills," *Sensible Regulations*, January 15, 2015, http://www.sensibleregulations.org/2015/01/nfib-declares-support-for-two-new-house-bills/.

61 "Washington Examiner: 27 regs for every new law," *Sensible Regulations*, January 5, 2015, http://www.sensibleregulations.org/2015/01/washington-examiner-27-regs-for-every-new-law/.

62 Michael Snyder, "12 ridiculous government regulations that are almost too bizarre to believe," *Business Insider*, November 12, 2010, http://www.businessinsider.com/ridiculous-regulations-big-government-2010-11.

- In the state of Texas, every new computer repair technician is required to have a degree in criminal justice or obtain a private investigator license (something about snooping in your data while they clean up the hard drive). Not many computer repair technicians have degrees in criminal justice, let's face it, or they probably wouldn't be working as computer repair technicians. The burden to get a PI license is enough to make anyone turn to drug dealing; a three-year apprenticeship with an already-licensed PI. Violators can be fined up to $4,000 and one year in jail. Lest you as a regular Josephine help your niece earn money for school by letting her repair the family computer, the law applies to you as well; you and your niece could both be in the pokey on graduation day.

- Love this. Massachusetts day care centers are mandated to make all children brush their teeth after lunch; the state will even provide the toothpaste, fluoride of course. I'm wondering if any of these state regulators have ever tried to make toddlers brush their teeth…in a line…in a public place…while simultaneously maintaining the safety and managing the behavior of the other children. I foresee two huge impediments to the regulation's implementation: 1) parents who claim a religious right for their children to enjoy "fuzzy sweaters" (AKA plaque) on their teeth could tie this up in the courts indefinitely; and 2) failure of staff to comply with the regulation could prompt visits from Child Protective Services and charges of child abuse. We'll see how this one goes.

- Michigan can fine/will fine/threatens to fine residents of Lake Elmo $1000 and put them in jail for 90 days if they sell pumpkins or Christmas trees grown outside the city limits. (Not really so ridiculous when compared to the first two, but that's not saying much.)

- Talk about kicking a girl when she's down. If you want to close a business in Milwaukee, Wisconsin, you have to obtain an expensive "going out of business license," and pay an additional fee based on the length of your "going out of business sale" plus $2 for every $1000 of inventory you are attempting to sell off.

- Some do-gooders have gotten the FDA to require that all products sold in vending machines be labeled with a calorie count that is visible to the consumer. (Personally, I don't want to know, thank you very much.) The food service industry estimates it will have to spend an additional 14 million hours every year to comply with this rain-on-our-parade regulation.

All of the above regulations are focused on small business, but there are other, less ridiculous yet still more burdensome regulations that apply to all businesses. As you would expect, it is much (much) easier[63] for large, established businesses to comply with new regulations because they often have experience in dealing with regulators; with that experience, they can find better and cheaper ways to implement new regulations.

Many regulations are "fixed cost," meaning they cost the same for a business with five or 500 employees—OSHA requirements, for example. Smaller businesses, which are usually less established, face a higher cost of implementation. If they are forced to raise prices to cover the increased cost, they risk becoming less competitive in the market.

Some regulations are virtually impossible for small business to comply with. Take the example of OSHA[64], which requires that all businesses have

---

63   Scott Shane, "To help small business, cut regulation," *Entrepreneur*, January 10, 2014. http://www.entrepreneur.com/article/230727.

64   "Is rising small business regulation driving down business formation?" *Small Business Trends*, January 10, 2014, http://smallbiztrends.com/2015/01/rising-small-business-regulation.html.

an injury and illness prevention program and *is considering a requirement that the plan address all foreseeable hazards* [emphasis added]. Foreseeable hazards in a factory, or even an office building, are fairly predictable and manageable. Any accident that could occur in home-based business, no matter how unlikely, could be interpreted as foreseeable, exposing the business to significant financial penalties. Knowing my kids and my pets, the list of potential injuries and illnesses is infinite. Were I running a business out of my home, it would be impossible for me to fully comply with this requirement in any reasonable way.

Small businesses that are not home-based may not fare much better. In 2010, a woman-owned painting business in Louisiana was forced to implement new safety precautions when working around lead-based paint. Employees were required to take government certification classes and wear expensive special goggles and coveralls, rubber gloves and hoods. The extra paperwork and purchase of equipment added thousands of dollars to the cost of doing business; she was financially ruined, the business lost two-thirds of its customers, and she was forced to lay off employees.

Third-party requirements increase the financial burden on small businesses indirectly. The Department of Labor is considering a new regulation[65] regarding labor-relations counsel, which is currently excluded from reporting under federal labor laws. Should the DOL adopt the proposed regulation, attorneys and firms offering labor-relations counsel would be required to disclose their fees and any arrangements with clients. Given the extra burden, many may no longer take on clients seeking labor-relations counsel. Meanwhile, large companies usually have in-house legal advice so there would be no net impact to them.

---

65 Ibid.

Even zoning laws can hurt small businesses[66], which are less likely than larger businesses to operate in commercially zoned locations. A family farm that wishes to sell Christmas trees may be in a zone that requires proceeds from trees sold in their front yard be donated to a non-profit entity. Good fences make good neighbors, but if you store supplies at your house that could potentially bother your neighbors, it's too bad for you. In some homeowners associations, a home-based lawn care business would not be allowed to store fertilizer or gas on-site if neighbors object.

Small businesses provide 55 percent[67] of all jobs today and have provided 66 percent of all net new jobs for the last 35 years. Regulation is a killer for the formation, expansion, and job creation of such businesses in an already sluggish economy. Would somebody please do some Stage 2 thinking?

Small businesses provide 55 percent of all jobs today and have provided 66 percent of all net new jobs for the last 35 years. Regulation is a killer for the formation, expansion, and job creation of such businesses in an already sluggish economy. Would somebody please do some Stage 2 thinking?

---

66   Carmen Nobel, "Banning big-box stores can hurt local retailers," *Forbes*, 07/07/2014, http://www.forbes.com/sites/hbsworkingknowledge/2014/07/07/banning-big-box-stores-can-hurt-local-retailers/#55189a4d4763.

67   "Gun Control Laws," Legal Match, accessed November 10, 2015, http://www.legal-match.com/law-library/article/gun-control-laws.html.

There are ways Congress[68] could break the leviathan's hold.

- Benchmark other countries to see how they have minimized their own business regulations.

- Require all federal agencies to seek approval of Congress before putting major regulations into effect.

- Attach expiration dates to all regulations so that out-of-date regulations are retired, and bureaucrats are compelled to actively renew regulations they wish to preserve.

The National Federation of Independent Business has suggested[69] allowing public participation in shaping regulations before government agencies propose them, and requiring agencies to choose the least costly regulatory option unless public health and safety would be adversely affected.

We need a president who sees the big picture and works to improve the economy by unstrangling small businesses from over regulation. Mr. or Madam President could start by making phone calls to OSHA and the DOL. Surely they have something better to do than choke the American economy to death.

We need a president who sees the big picture and works to improve the economy by unstrangling small businesses from over regulation.

---

68 Scott Shane, "To help small business, cut regulation," *Entrepreneur*, January 10, 2014. http://www.entrepreneur.com/article/230727.

69 "NFIB declares support for two new House bills," *Sensible Regulations*, January 15, 2015, http://www.sensibleregulations.org/2015/01/nfib-declares-support-for-two-new-house-bills/.

FISCAL RESPONSIBILITY

Will the candidate make tough, politically unpopular choices?

Tax policy is shaping up to be one of the major issues of the 2016 presidential campaign," says the non-profit Tax Foundation[70], which maintains a regularly updated list of 2016 presidential tax reform proposals.

"Maybe," says I. The candidates need to be vetted for their proposed plans of course, but if we have another San Bernardino a month before the election, tax reform will take a distant—far distant—second to national security and public safety. When the house is on fire, you don't worry about balancing the checkbook.

When the house is on fire, you don't worry about balancing the checkbook.

---

70   The website for Tax Foundation, TaxFoundation.org

Even though it might not end up being a voting issue, it's a good way to assess the candidate's overall competence. Kind of like we don't really elect a vice-president, but it pays to be aware that s/he is next in line.

The best place to start understanding fiscal responsibility is to connect the dots between our economy and many of the foregoing issues; immigration, small business regulation, the "war on women," and terrorism. A good example is the Congressional Budget Office's finding that President Obama's 2016 budget[71] "would make U.S. output larger over the next decade than it would be under current law—*mostly by changing immigration laws* [emphasis added]."

Immigration

President Obama intends to increase the size of the labor force to boost tax receipts and spending for federal benefit programs. There's a certain elegance to such a simple solution, but the real world is hardly ever simple, much less elegant. Much depends on the skill level of the immigrants who arrive to make President Obama's desired economic enlargement.

Engineers, doctors, and other H1-B visa immigrants will both help the economy with their taxes and potentially contribute to technological advances. If, however, a higher proportion of new immigrants are low-skilled and command lower wages, average wages across the entire labor force go down. And, just as with American citizens, the lower the skill level, the higher the likelihood of dependence on government programs like Food Stamps and Section 8 Housing.

The Center for Immigration Studies[72] estimates that 87 percent of

---

71 "A macroeconomic analysis of the President's 2016 budget, *Congressional Budget Office*, August 21, 2014, https://www.cbo.gov/publication/50734.

72 The website for Center for Immigration Studies, Cis.org

immigrant households (legal and illegal) in 2012 had at least one worker, yet 51 percent of that 87 percent were unable to provide for their basic needs and relied on one or more welfare programs. Some immigrants are a net positive, some are a financial net negative. A budget that calls for increased revenues from people who may cost the system more than they benefit it is a roll of the dice at best.

Business Regulation

Business regulation costs the economy more than it saves the economy; when it's a matter of public safety and well-being, the money is well spent. When excessive business regulation arises from special interest groups or elitist pet notions, it takes money from the collective kitty, forcing small business owners to close their doors or lay off employees.

President Obama's "plan[73] to create a 21st century regulatory system" includes somewhat vague reforms that promise the elimination of "tens of millions of hours of paperwork." A shell game if we recall that the food industry expects to spend 14 million more hours every year to comply with newly imposed government paperwork. So, is this a net positive or a net negative?

President Obama's proposed reforms are either vague or tricky on purpose. His plan proclaims that "government agencies have identified over 580 proposals to reduce regulatory costs." I've identified that I have a problem with Krispy Kremes; I have no real intention of doing anything about it. Telling us that government agencies have identified proposals tells us nothing about the ensuing action items, if any.

---

73 "Jobs & the economy: Putting America back to work," *The White House*, accessed January 1, 2016, https://www.whitehouse.gov/economy/reform.

President Obama's proposed reforms are either vague or tricky on purpose. His plan proclaims that "government agencies have identified over 580 proposals to reduce regulatory costs." I've identified that I have a problem with Krispy Kremes; I have no real intention of doing anything about it. Telling us that government agencies have identified proposals tells us nothing about the ensuing action items, if any.

The War on Women

The war on women is defined primarily as an attack on women's reproductive freedom and choices. It's embarrassing to be identified with middle class women who demand government subsidies for their birth control, but no one disputes that some women rely on subsidized healthcare overall. You can come down on the pro-life-pro-choice continuum anywhere you like; just be aware that subsidizing poor women's abortions by funding extra-governmental agencies (Planned Parenthood) is a taxpayer expense and affects every other part of the economy.

It's embarrassing to be identified with middle class women who demand government subsidies for their birth control, but no one disputes that some women rely on subsidized healthcare overall.

Terrorism

Threats to homeland security, foreign or domestic, always trigger more spending. I'm not a betting woman, but if I were, my money would be on a steady increase in terrorist attacks on American soil going forward. We'll spend the money to protect the public for sure, but where will that money come from? The only money the government has to protect us is the money it takes from us to fund itself. Our collective wallet has only so much money, and what if taxes become such a burden that it's no longer worth it to work as hard. (See Laffer Curve[74].) If we kill the goose that lays the golden egg, how much power will we have to protect ourselves?

The only money the government has to protect us is the money it takes from us to fund itself.

I hate to tell you, but the golden goose is already headed for the chopping block. The horrifyingly, nauseatingly up-to-the-minute national debt clock[75] spins so fast, you can hardly register the numbers. At 12:42:00 on January 14, 2015, it calculated our total debt to be $18,810,620,484,399. That's a debt per citizen burden of $58,277, and a debt per taxpayer burden of $157,205. By the time I finished writing that sentence, our debt had increased by almost $3 million.

---

74 "The Laffer Curve shows that tax increases are a very bad idea — even if they generate more tax revenue," *Forbes*, April 15, 2012, http://www.forbes.com/sites/danielmitchell/2012/04/15/the-laffer-curve-shows-that-tax-increases-are-a-very-bad-idea-even-if-they-generate-more-tax-revenue/#5e7652116307.

75 The website for U.S. Debt Clock; USDebtClock.org

The golden goose is already headed for the chopping block. The horrifyingly, nauseatingly up-to-the-minute national debt clock spins so fast, you can hardly register the numbers. At 12:42:00 on January 14, 2015, it calculated our total debt to be $18,810,620,484,399. That's a debt per citizen burden of $58,277, and a debt per taxpayer burden of $157,205. By the time I finished writing that sentence, our debt had increased by almost $3 million.

Since 2010, eight U.S cities and one county—Jefferson County, AL—have filed for bankruptcy, one-third of those municipalities in California alone. Detroit filed for Chapter 9 relief on July 18, 2013, making it the largest municipal bankruptcy filing in U.S. history by debt (estimated at $18-20 billion).

There go fire stations, fire fighters, and police, which means increased response time for emergencies. Maintenance of roads is put on hold, city workers' pay and benefits are cut, and "death-by-pension" has won: the slow takeover of retirement benefits for police, firefighters, highway patrol, police, prison guards, billboard inspectors, school security guards, cooks at prisons, even lifeguards.

The U.S. government's credit rating was lowered for the first time in history on August 5, 2011. Like homeowners pay higher interest on a mortgage when their credit is poor, the U.S. is now exposed to higher interest on the massive debt we owe to other countries. There is a congressional limit to the amount of debt we're allowed to carry, but that doesn't seem to slow us down for long. The limit was raised in October 2015 for the 74th time since

1962. And when Congress does try to curb spending, cries of government shutdown, e.g., forcing little old ladies on Social Security to go without heat, makes it near impossible.

The good news, which is only good news when we don't expect much from Congress, is that Standard and Poor "affirmed" our lower credit rating[76] for the next two years. "Mr. and Mrs. Taxpayer, you now pay higher interest because of dings to your credit, and you get to do so for at least two more years."

And the granddaddy of all golden goose killers? Social Security, a safety net begun in 1935 with 1935-era vision. We were in the middle of the Great Depression, average retirement age was 65, and average life expectancy was 61. Social insurance to protect ourselves and our families from loss of income at retirement seemed like a good idea at the time. Started with the best of intentions, it now paves our road to financial ruin.

During the baby boom, high birth rates produced 159.4 workers paying into the system for each retiree drawing out of the system. Today there are 2.8 workers for each retiree, and life expectancy is 78.7. Since 2010, the total of Social Security employee taxes coming in minus the total of benefit payments going out is a negative number. Social Security has become the largest benefit program in the world and is projected to run out of money by 2034.

(Fun fact: Social Security benefits are entitlements, not legally required payments. Yesterday's Congress designed Social Security as an insurance system to return to retirees the money they paid into the fund over their working careers; today's Congress can change the rules at any time. If they don't change them soon, there won't be anything left to worry about.)

---

76   "S&P affirms U.S. AA+ credit rating, maintains stable outlook," *Bloomberg News*, June 10, 2015, http://www.bloomberg.com/news/articles/2015-06-10/s-p-affirms-u-s-aa-credit-rating-maintains-stable-outlook.

It's our children and grandchildren who will pay the price for today's lack of fiscal responsibility, a price they are already paying. For the first time in our history, the rising generation will not rise higher than the one that came before. We are borrowing the dollars today that future generations will have to repay tomorrow, and their national wallet will carry even less cash in it than ours does, thanks to our unwillingness to say "no" to more (and more) spending. It's time to push back from the money table. It's time to take one for the younger team.

AARP (the American Association of Retired Persons) could have been instrumental in helping to reform Social Security so that benefits were still available for future retirees; they didn't. Their powerful lobby spent $25 million in the 2012 presidential election cycle and $16 million during the 2014 midterm elections to protect today's retirees at the expense of tomorrow's families. There was no one to stop them. Millennials haven't had time to develop the kind of entrenched political apparatus that the older generation uses to great advantage. Millennials don't even vote in large numbers.

It's not too late to give the golden goose CPR, but it has to hurt now or it won't work. Raising the age for collecting Social Security benefits and reducing the benefit amounts for people under 55 makes so much sense, but it's unpopular with older citizens who are the most likely to vote and therefore have the most political clout[77]. One frustrated 25-year-old said, "Our generation has grown up with full acceptance of crushing debt. We might not care as much as we should because we've never known life without it."

Well, the rest of us know life without it. If young people don't have the ability to see around corners, or the power to do anything about it if they

---

77 "Emily Brandon, "Why older citizens are more likely to vote," *U.S. News and World Report*, March 19, 2012, http://money.usnews.com/money/retirement/articles/2012/03/19/why-older-citizens-are-more-likely-to-vote.

could, we do. Are we really going to sell future generations down the river because it's not our problem? That's not very American.

We have to hold ourselves and our candidates responsible for showing integrity today, for making hard choices and painful sacrifices to right our economic shipwreck of an economy. We got ourselves and our children and our grandchildren into this mess; we owe them some help getting out of it. More and more entitlements set the mouth to watering, but the next president must be strong enough to make necessary cutbacks. We need a president with the strength and vision to lead us in the politically unpopular path of restoring health to our economy.

We have to hold ourselves and our candidates responsible for showing integrity today, for making hard choices and painful sacrifices to right our economic shipwreck of an economy. We got ourselves and our children and our grandchildren into this mess; we owe them some help getting out of it.

CONCLUSION

Lots of issues are thrown around during a presidential campaign: terrorism, illegal immigration, abortion, extra-terrestrials[78], and so on. A solid vetting of the candidates begins with a solid understanding of which issues are real and which are distractions. Evaluate only those issues the candidate can influence.

Lots of issues are thrown around during a presidential campaign. Evaluate only those issues the candidate can influence.

No matter who is in office, Roe v. Wade isn't going anywhere; the war on women is a hat trick. Solving the illegal immigration crisis will necessarily be a torturous compromise between many interested parties; balancing the budget and addressing the Syrian (and inevitably other) refugee crisis likewise. The areas in which a president can exert real influence are foreign policy, small business regulation, terrorism, parents' relationship to their children, free speech and microaggressions. Spend your time evaluating candidates on these issues.

---

78   Kate Scanlon, "Hillary Clinton vows to 'get to the bottom' of what's in Area 51," *The Blaze*, January 4, 2016, http://www.theblaze.com/stories/2016/01/04/hillary-clinton-vows-to-get-to-the-bottom-of-whats-in-area-51/.

**Roe v. Wade isn't going anywhere;
the war on women is a hat trick.**

Not so much areas of influence as keys to character, the candidates' attitudes toward American exceptionalism, the Constitution, and the rule of law reveal what makes them tick. For me, this is the most important area of evaluation. Once we have a grasp of who each candidate is as a person, evaluating the issues of the day is a straightforward check on their integrity.

Keys to character, the candidates' attitudes toward American exceptionalism, the Constitution, and the rule of law reveal what makes them tick.

Finally, don't make perfect the enemy of the good. As the field stands today, we are each going to have to do some serious settling for a candidate we don't love but who is the lesser of evils. Do we cut off our arms, our legs, or our ears? I've never understood people who opt out of voting because they don't like their choices. Somebody is still elected, still vetoes bills, and still appoints Supreme Court justices. And if we're subject to a president's influence on our lives, don't we have a responsibility to weigh in on the selection?

As the field stands today, we are each going to have to do some serious settling for a candidate we don't love but who is the lesser of evils. Do we cut off our arms, our legs, or our ears?

Decide where you stand on the issues. Look at where the candidates stand. Evaluate the candidates as people. Cast an informed vote. And, as always, *read widely and think for yourself.*